LONDON
SHITE

LONDON SHITE

QUALITY-FREE JOURNALISM

Published in 2009 by New Holland Publishers (UK) Ltd
London • Cape Town • Sydney • Auckland
www.newhollandpublishers.com
Garfield House, 86–88 Edgware Road, London W2 2EA, United Kingdom
80 McKenzie Street, Cape Town 8001, South Africa
Unit 1, 66 Gibbes Street, Chatswood, NSW 2067, Australia
218 Lake Road, Northcote, Auckland, New Zealand

10 9 8 7 6 5 4 3 2 1

A catalogue record for this book is available from the British Library

ISBN 978 1 84773 489 1

Senior Editor: Kate Parker
Publishing Direction: Rosemary Wilkinson
Publisher: Aruna Vasudevan
Design Manager: David Etherington Design
Design: London Shite
Cover Design: David Etherington Design
Production: Melanie Dowland

Reproduction by PDQ Digital Media Solutions Ltd, UK
Printed and bound in Singapore by Craft Print International Ltd, Singapore

CONTENT PLANNER

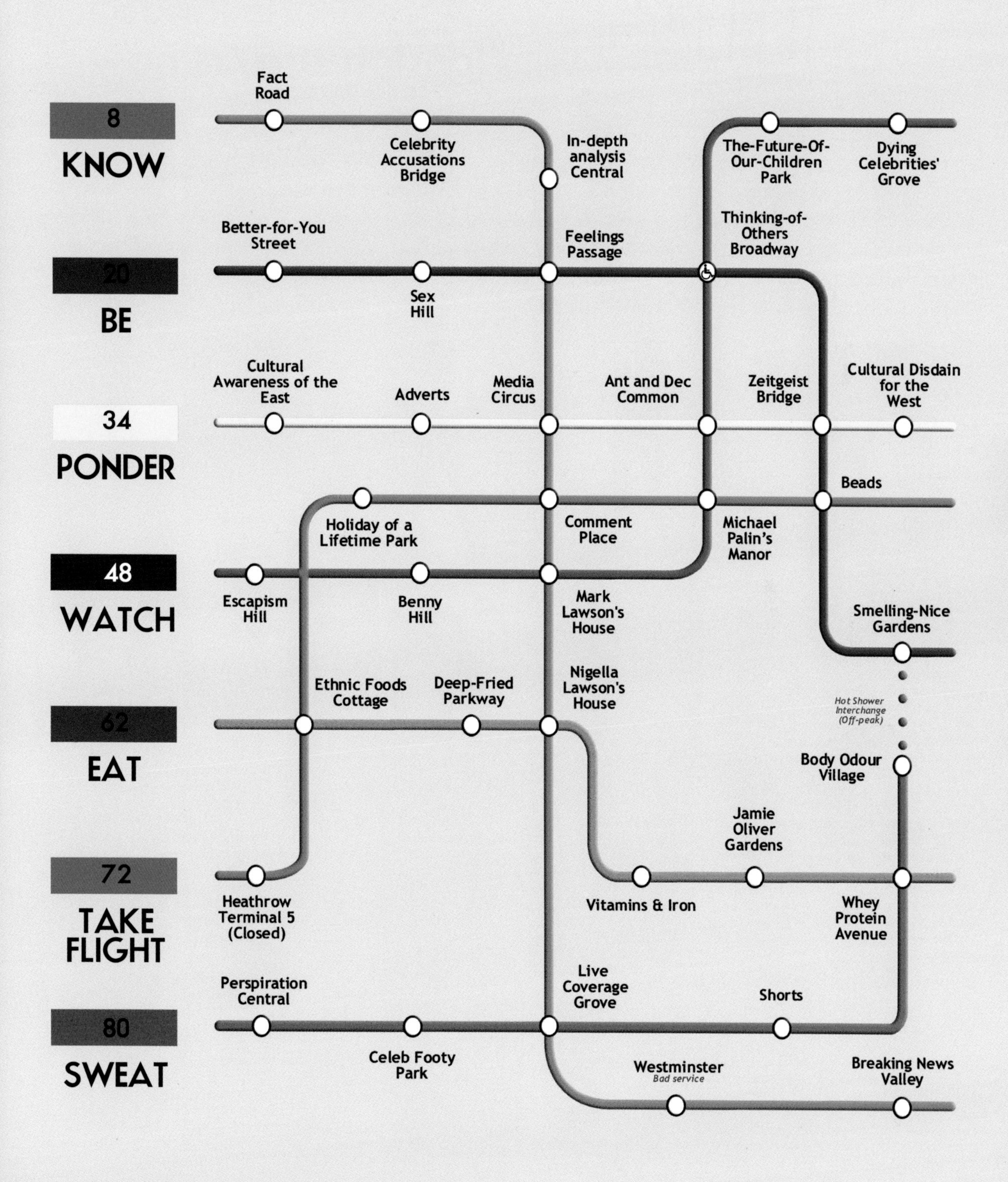

{ethos}

this is london.
we are london.
we/london are/is now.

Since 9/11, now has taken on an even greater urgency. As Londoners we are privileged to experience the cultural vertigo of being on the cusp of now. We like to think of London-Shite as the media epicentre of now-culture. Our aim is to provide Londoners with up-to-date trends as they are created, imagined (re-imagined?) and immediatized. From warhol to Winton, Titian to Titchmarsh - we cock no snooks. It's a little concept we like to call 'omni-culture'.

WHO ARE WE?
WE ARE
WHERE IS IT?
LONDON
WHY?
SEE ABOVE
FOREVER?
YES

RUPERT ATATAT
EDITOR

Rupert is no stranger to the bustle of an editor's office, having founded and dissolved over 50 publications including The Squatter, Tribal Art Review, and the cult fashion magazines Plimp, Jaxi and Torrid. Having lived through most of the major events of the 21st Century from 9/11 to the comeback of Noel Edmonds, Rupert brings a unique editorial perspective to our publication. He mingles with the great and the good most weekends, and once exchanged insurance details with Nelson Mandela He lives with his partner Patricia and their highland terrier, Brecht.

CHAD ALTERCATION
CONCEPT ACTIONER

Chad is a multi-talented creative who has lived and worked in London since leaving St Paul's Boys School with straight As. His ---mantra has long been "London is my canvas, and words are my easel", and it is that nebulous way of thinking that keeps London Shite fresh and ahead of the crowd. Prior to joining our team, Chad was one of the most sought after stars of advertising agency St Binsey & Steiner, and was responsible for Cadbury's notorious "Gorilla pissing in a cup" TV adverts. Outside of work he designs his own T-shirts and rides a BMX really fast.

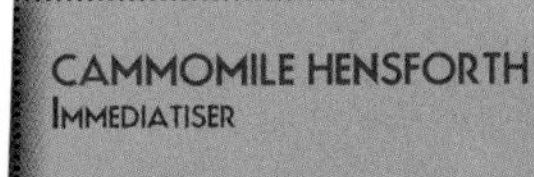

CAMMOMILE HENSFORTH
IMMEDIATISER

Cammomile has travelled the world from Thailand to Australia, and brought a whole new international perspective to London Shite when we recruited her. She wears many beads. She's a "Yes" girl, always up for new experiences, and has slept with several illegal taxi drivers in the last decade. She is also famed for her charity work – she is a passionate supporter of Gaelic rights, and after 7/7 opened her flat in Chelsea to survivors to offer them support and lobster bisque. Cammomile currently lives in Shoreditch with a Turkish man who makes and sells drums.

JESSY 'TITSI' FUNNELL
SHOWBIZ FAIRY

The love child of the receptionist at the Groucho Club and an unidentifiable member of The Stone Roses, Jessy has grown up in and amongst celebs and their favourite spots giving her unique access to the world of 'shine and dazzle' that brings something unique to London Shite. Jessy is the co-author of 'High-Humidity Yoga - the T4 way' and is a keen campaigner for better labelling on vegan ready-meals.

MICK DICKS
SAD NEWS UNRAVELLER

Born into relative penury on the wrong side of Primrose Hill, Mick's tough upbringing amongst immigrants and living directly opposite a council estate for over 3 years has given him a gritty take on the searing world of rotten London that few of us really want but all of us enjoy dipping into. He has made over 7 pilots for Bravo about the darker side of our capital and is a keen and unrepentant smoker.

How We London Shite

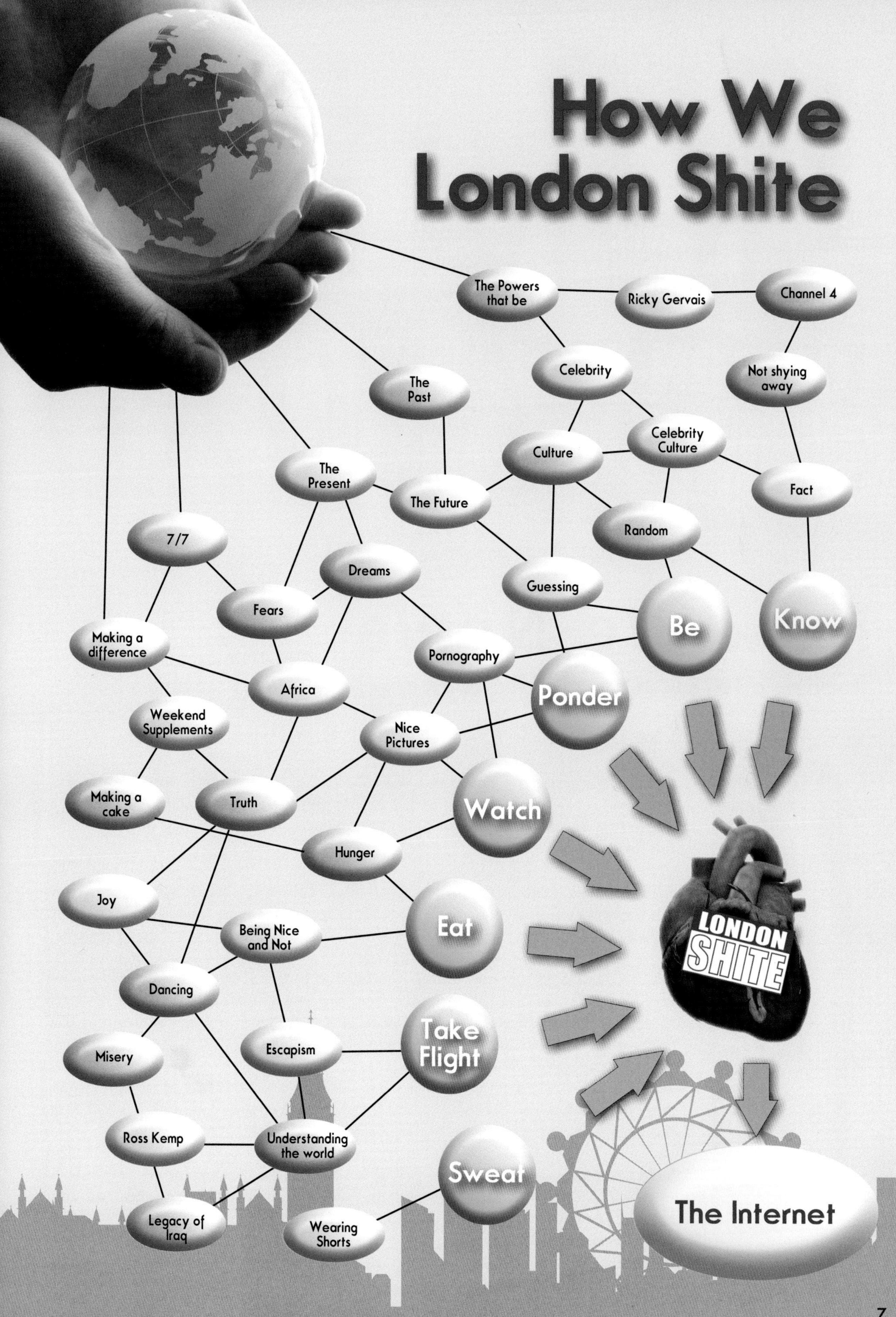

How We News

Readers often ask us just how the Shite news cycle works. Here's how:

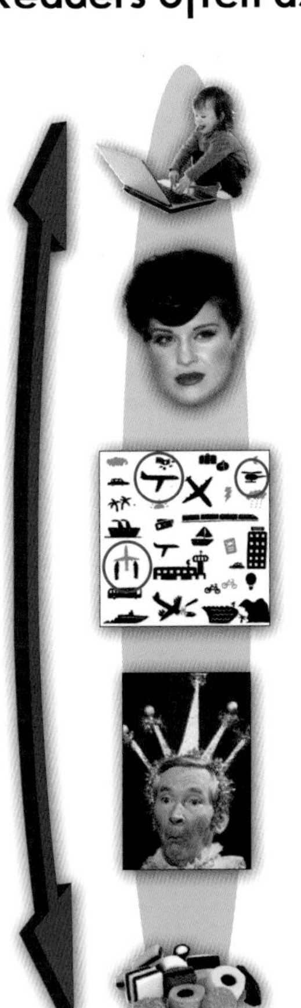

OUR UNIQUE **FLANGE** STRATEGY...

FIND – We scour the BBC news website for up to 8 hours a day, looking for hot news, gossip, and funny or distressing pictures. Within minutes of a story appearing, the Shite team are already thinking about potentially getting it into the next issue.

LEARN – The team get together over a bruschetta to discuss what they think the news is really about, often consulting top celebs and cultural personalities, including Kelly Osborne and Uri Geller, to determine the relevance of a story.

ACTION – Reporters and editors are hurried to the scene in special rucksacks carried by the London Shite interns. They then disembark and use their iPhones to digitise and condense the event into no more than 3 easily comprehensible concepts from Microsoft's ClipArt image gallery.

RE**N**EW(S) – Our specialist editors give each story an angle to keep it fresh and unique, such as replacing every full stop with a question mark or rewriting the item with the voice and tone of Kenneth Williams.

GALVANISE – Printed editions are given to our 250,000 immigrant distributors at a warehouse in London's Docklands. They are invigorated with hot tea and rousing music before being released onto the capital's streets.

EMPATHISE – For every 10,000 copies deployed, each distributor receives a packet of Liquorice Allsorts.

Political Event of The Year

Barry O Fun

Without doubt the stand-out happening on the political calendar was the opening of the new Barack Obama theme park – offering acres and acres of fizzy rhetoric across four inspirationally titled 'zones'.

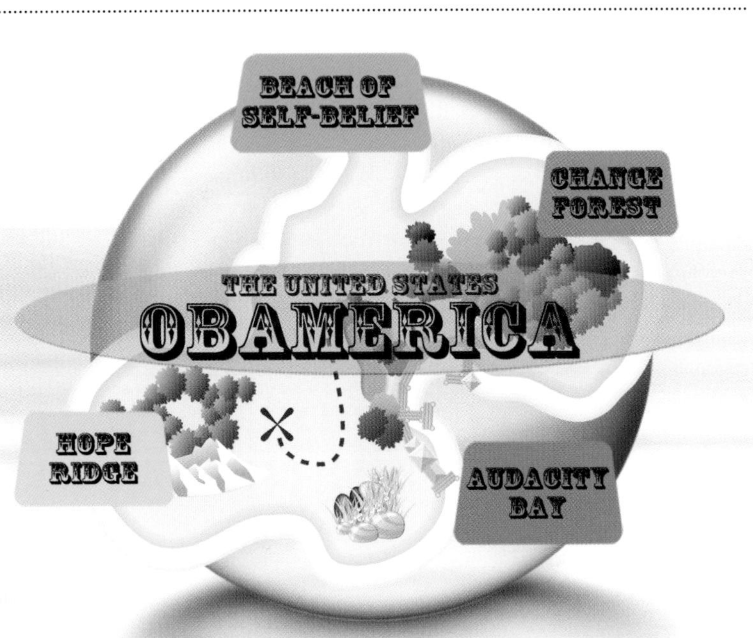

JUST CHECK OUT THE RIDES!

The African Descent

This is the ride everyone's been talking about. Its light safari theming makes it seem wildly exotic and impossibly daring, despite the fact it's essentially no different from most other log flumes. The ride itself is surprisingly comfortable, with most of the journey spent drifting through a mock-up of the Harvard Law School library, receiving occassionally comptempuous looks from staff and colleagues.

Race Mountain

If you love Obama to bits but just can't fully empathise with his ethnic tribulations as much as you'd like, why not have a go at scaling the mighty Race Mountain? Every step closer to the summit reveals an exciting chapter in the history of the Civil Rights movement carved into the rock, but your path to the top is constantly hampered through no fault of your own. Will you make it all the way?

Barack To The Future

For anyone getting impatient about the whole global mess being sorted out, just take a step inside Barack To The Future. Once buckled into your DeLorean, a Doc Brown look-alike injects you with a heady combo of drugs designed to render you comfortably unconscious until Barry's tidied up. When you eventually come round, the world will be all better again!

SNAP, CRACKLE AND CRUNCH

Remember when we used to be picky about the balsamic vinegar we bought? All that changed when the layers of global credit that hold financial institutions and money markets in place began to subside and literally 'crunch' into one another. Here we present our guide to all things Crunch and ponder the seminality of specific crunchy moments.

THOU SHALT NOT FRITTER

Crunch-stopper General Alistair Darling invoked some centuries-old statutes designed to maximise London's dwindling supply of economic vitality and also show remorse to the Lord for all our sloth and greed...

1. All top hats must be worn 24 hours a day to give the illusion of economic grandeur thus frightening off the spirits of Crunch.

2. The first born of each London family to be sent into Epping forest to hunt fruit and trap small birds for food lest the capital's diminishing supply of victuals be damaged.

3. To boost productivity and ensure maximum national anti-Crunch effort, infamous social pariahs are to be brought back into the fold of British society. John Leslie will cut logs for fire in Arbroath whilst Gary Glitter will drive old people to the sea.

4. Sea water to be drunk at all times – Crunch-stopper Darling firmly believes that our current plague is caused by London's four choleric humours being out of balance. The cold saltiness of sea water can revive melancholy, which must then be balanced in the phlegmatic humour with a sticky bun or a bottle of Yop.

5. Pets to be abandoned or fought against one another as a value-laden entertainment spectacle offered in lieu of expensive Premiership football.

6. The Chanson de Mort – a macabre 14th-century dance – to be performed by every Londoner each Friday at dusk to scare away the ghosts of Crunch. Each borough of London will be assigned a T4 presenter to arrange, cajole and lead the dance.

What Is Money? And How Does It Work, Please?

The Markets Explained

We were all affected by the Downturn™, but how many of us knew exactly what was going on beyond what Huw Edwards told us? Internalising our simple flow diagram meant people understood exactly what was happening to their money.

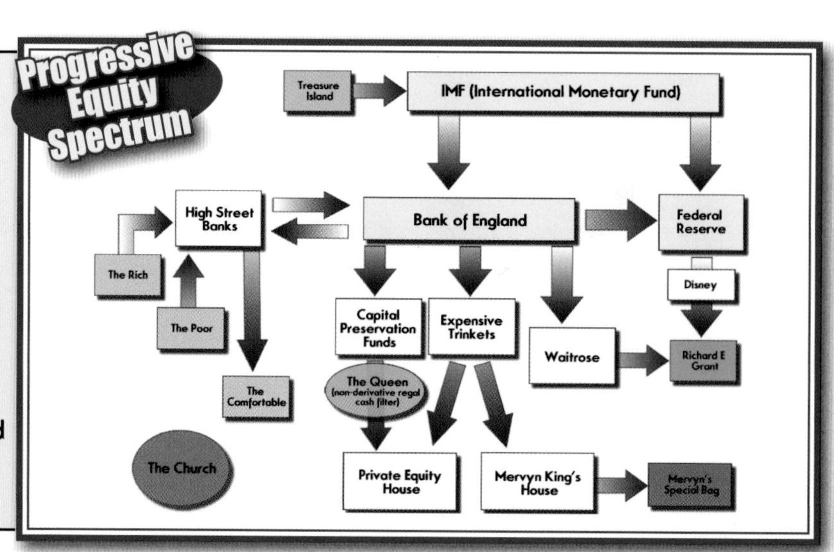

CRA$H COUR$E

For the more advanced crunchee, we also provided this breakdown of some of the key vocabulary found in financial chatrooms:

SUPRA-TRADING – While we hear of everything that happens in the markets during working hours, it is the trading that goes on after hours that is most influential and most erratic. This is known as supra-trading. Bankers will often drunkenly exchange shares after their day's work, and have been known to lose them in the backs of taxis on the journey home. The practice only came to light in 2001 when one city worker offered bar staff the Dutch conglomerate Reed Elsevier in return for a cheese ploughman's.

WHORE-ISH MARKET – We are currently in a whore-ish market, called such because the weakened pound is "going down on the dollar". The opposite of a whore-ish market is a Princely Market. Occasionally an economy can reach a point of stasis in which it is neither growing nor shrinking, causing months of extraordinarily boring trading conditions. This is known as the Mark Lawrenson Effect.

SPONTANEOUS LIQUID DEVALUATION – SLD occurs when a trader has sold so much stock in a company that he or she is sick down him- or herself, and hence rendered unfit for trading. The collapse of Lehman Brothers was a result of multiple SLDs within the space of a few minutes. Also known as "Chunkinomics".

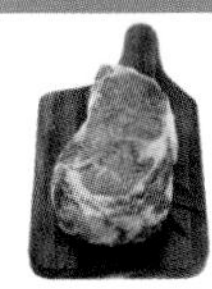

MEAT-BASED UNCLARITY LOSSES – Any loss of market value that stems from confusion over whether a banker is talking about company stock or meat stock in any particular instance.

easyWomen

repulsive male?

not enough coin for phonebox callgirls?

easyWomen specialises in no frills hookers – no fancy business – just cheap, functional minge

featured easyWoman

MANDY, 39

5 euros/hr

The Crunch Bunch: Our Top Three Crunch-busting Investments

Bratz "My Robert Peston" Doll

If your kids are already fans of the Bratz craze, they'll have great fun with this 6-inch Peston replica. Pull the tiny analyst's tie to hear him berate your little terrors for their wayward consumerism and offer constructive advice on saving for the future.

RSC's Bargain Bucket at the Globe Theatre

A season of semi-competent Elizabethan theatre in which actors from Eastenders, Holby City and The Bill enact the few lines they can remember from previous Shakespeare productions they have been in or have auditioned for in the past.

Howard "Halifax" Brown's Shocking Autobiography

Promising readers "a gripping read with a high rate of interest" this inspirational rags-to-riches tale reveals Howard's life in quite astonishing detail. More than just a book, 'You Can Bank On It!' also includes full scale step charts and a sing-along DVD so you and your friends can recreate all Howard's classic TV routines.

Google Launches 'Population Clock'

Stat-lovers and fact-fetishists warmly received Google's plans for a new Population Clock application, which will provide a real-time counter for absolutely everything on Planet Earth. As well as constantly updating the total human population, internet globaphiles will also be able to monitor everything from births and deaths to the total number of people currently wearing a hat.

Responsible parents of the West! Prepare your children for a world free from violence with...

DIPLOMACY MAN

INSTIL JOY IN YOUR YOUNG AS THEIR SURE-FOOTED PACIFISTIC DOLL NEGOTIATES A SAFER WORLD FOR THE ENTIRE PLAYROOM.

MARVEL AS DIPLOMACY MAN...

- calms a querolous press conference with the lowering of his right hand
- distributes velcro 'hearts and minds'
- paces the room exuding hope

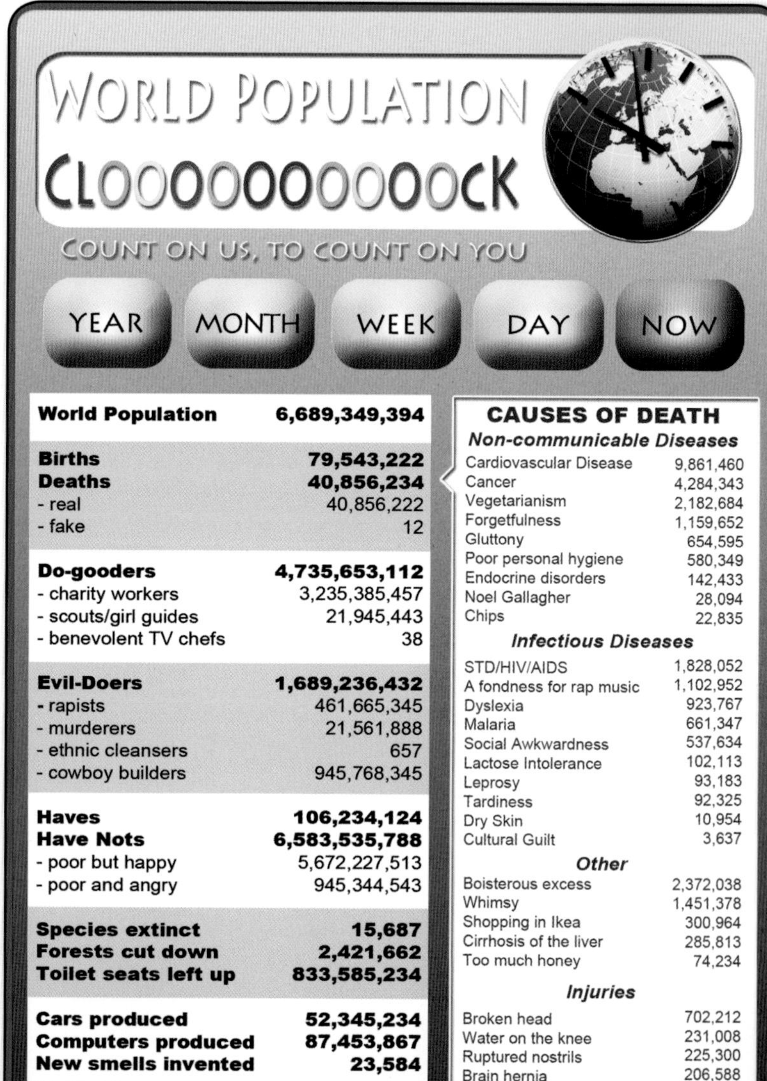

WORLD POPULATION CLOOOOOOOOOOCK

COUNT ON US, TO COUNT ON YOU

YEAR | MONTH | WEEK | DAY | NOW

World Population	**6,689,349,394**
Births	**79,543,222**
Deaths	**40,856,234**
- real	40,856,222
- fake	12
Do-gooders	**4,735,653,112**
- charity workers	3,235,385,457
- scouts/girl guides	21,945,443
- benevolent TV chefs	38
Evil-Doers	**1,689,236,432**
- rapists	461,665,345
- murderers	21,561,888
- ethnic cleansers	657
- cowboy builders	945,768,345
Haves	**106,234,124**
Have Nots	**6,583,535,788**
- poor but happy	5,672,227,513
- poor and angry	945,344,543
Species extinct	**15,687**
Forests cut down	**2,421,662**
Toilet seats left up	**833,585,234**
Cars produced	**52,345,234**
Computers produced	**87,453,867**
New smells invented	**23,584**
Keys lost	**267,345,345**
- in other pocket	213,534,234
- down back of sofa	54,235,662
Keys found	**456,234,634**

CAUSES OF DEATH

Non-communicable Diseases	
Cardiovascular Disease	9,861,460
Cancer	4,284,343
Vegetarianism	2,182,684
Forgetfulness	1,159,652
Gluttony	654,595
Poor personal hygiene	580,349
Endocrine disorders	142,433
Noel Gallagher	28,094
Chips	22,835
Infectious Diseases	
STD/HIV/AIDS	1,828,052
A fondness for rap music	1,102,952
Dyslexia	923,767
Malaria	661,347
Social Awkwardness	537,634
Lactose Intolerance	102,113
Leprosy	93,183
Tardiness	92,325
Dry Skin	10,954
Cultural Guilt	3,637
Other	
Boisterous excess	2,372,038
Whimsy	1,451,378
Shopping in Ikea	300,964
Cirrhosis of the liver	285,813
Too much honey	74,234
Injuries	
Broken head	702,212
Water on the knee	231,008
Ruptured nostrils	225,300
Brain hernia	206,588
Shampoo in the eye	183,817
Accident at Laser Quest party	543,737
Stannah stairlift malfunction	515,174
Car Crash	329,364
War	100,962

When Do I Care?

With so many bad things going on in the world, it can be a nightmare to juggle your feelings of grief and self-righteousness with the kids and a career. Our handy CARE-endar revolutionised the entire altruism industry by helping people divide their empty feelings of concern more evenly so no one had to feel left out.

SYMPATHY TIMETABLE

- Cheesed Off
- Griefy
- Nearly in mourning
- Hopping mad

DAY	CRISIS	FEELING	LITTLE THOUGHT	ACTION
Mon	IRAQ AND THAT WHOLE AREA	Impatience	'Why can't it be better already?'	Write to BBC demanding more upbeat news
Tues	RACISM	Disgust	'Did the Lighthouse Family teach us nothing?'	Shake head slowly and buy every Lenny Henry DVD
Weds	DECLINE OF BRITISH FARMHOUSE CHEESES	Frustration	'What about the farmers?'	Boycott Primula
Thurs	POVERTY	Anger	'Why isn't it history yet?'	Laugh with a homeless person
Fri	THE ENVIRONMENT	Dejection	'Where is the bucolic idyll of my youth?'	Wear more hemp
Sat	LACK OF LOCAL YOUTH ACTIVITIES	Fury	'Will they stab me instead?'	Organise a 5-a-side match between rival gangs
Sun	THE LEGACY OF BRITAIN'S EMPIRE	Guilt	'Did I create Mugabe and his ilk?'	Go on safari to Kenya and look very apologetic

Now You Too Can Play God With...

In a bid to zazz up its antediluvian image in these thrillingly Godless times, the Church of England has released their brand new Fantasy Synod game, allowing you to put together your dream line-up for the C of E's very own governing body. Build up your Synod, build up your points and build up your kudos at work or in the playground. How will you spend your £100 million?

SEARCH: Bishops / Clergy / Laity RANGE: 5m - Any
DIOCESE: Any

PLAYER	HOLINESS	VALUE	SCORE
BISHOPS			
Archbishop of Canterbury	5	£33m	206
Archbishop of York	4	£26m	177
Bishop of Coventry	3	£18m	98
Bishop of Bristol	3	£19m	53
Bishop of Warwick	2	£12m	76
Bishop of Rochester	-3	£7.5m	-132
Bishop of Durham	4	£22m	56
Bishop of London	1	£8.7m	15
Bishop of Liverpool	3	£14m	76

ARCHBISHOP OF YORK

REAL NAME: Dr John Sentamu
AGE: 60
APPS: 117
CLEAN SHEETS: 12
BAPTISMS: 35
MARRIAGES: 12
PRAYERS: 74

£26m

ADD PLAYER?

Synod Value: £33m

In The Bank: £67m

SUBS

FORMATION
- V-WING
- OPEN
- MITRE
- VESTRY
- ORB
- CRUCIFIX
- ATTACK

Rules Of The Game

Construct your Fantasy Synod using your £100 million to buy any combination of 3 Bishops, 2 Clergy and 1 Layperson. You may not have more than 3 members of any one diocese in your Synod, and your cumulative holiness must be higher than 15 at all times. You are allowed 1 transfer per gameweek, except during Lent when transfers are suspended, and at Christmas when you are allowed up to 3. Excommunication for any player will score zero for that gameweek.

Scoring

Points are awarded as follows:

BISHOPS
- Concrete proof of God: +5
- Kind to the poor: +3
- Coronate a monarch: +2
- TV appearance: +1
- Sinful thought: -1
- Caught with hooker: -3

CLERGY
- Well-organised fete: +5
- 10+ in congregation: +2
- Sermon under 2hrs: +1
- Sex with choirboy: -3

LAITY
- Do Songs of Praise: +5
- Watch Songs of Praise: +3
- Record Songs of Praise: +1
- Miss Songs of Praise: -3

Kim Jong-Il 'Couldn't Be Less Dead' And Holiday Snaps 'Couldn't Be Less Fake'

North Korean officials reacted with outrage to suggestions that certain publicity shots of the Dear Leader might have been faked. The pictures, reportedly taken on a birthday trip to Pyongyang's MegaWaterHappyTown, show Kim enjoying himself silly on the slides, chilling out on a lilo, and even having a laugh with a fully-grown killer whale.

That's not a Knife! (Guide)

With knife crime rampaging almost past the point of no return on the capital's streets, we helped the Home Office launch this informational campaign based around popular kids game, Top Trumps. Aimed in equal measure at both disseminating official knife wisdom and keeping naughty hands busy with a thrilling new hobby, each card features a pointy thing regularly found during searches of ne'er-do-wells.

I ONLY KNOW THIS MUCH...

The Gift Of Celebrity Wisdom

Some experiential wisdom nuggets from ALEXA CHUNG

I've learnt everything I ever needed from Lou Reed and Wikipedia.
The Velvet Underground were like surrogate parents to me. I think music and instruments can convey more words than speech. But Wikipedia was really helpful when I did my GCSEs.

A cow cannot run.
It's something to do with the shape of their knees. I've never seen it proven otherwise.

Dermot O'Leary has the withered hands and wrists of an 80-year-old woman.
He won't thank me for saying that but I think honesty is really important, and I really value it.

I never put milk in an omelette.
If I do, it always falls to pieces when I take it out of the pan. I like to put ham in it.

Privatising the rail network was like a dagger in the heart of Britain's conscience.
I was very young when it happened, but look at the state we're in. When will politicians/businessmen realise it's not all about the money?

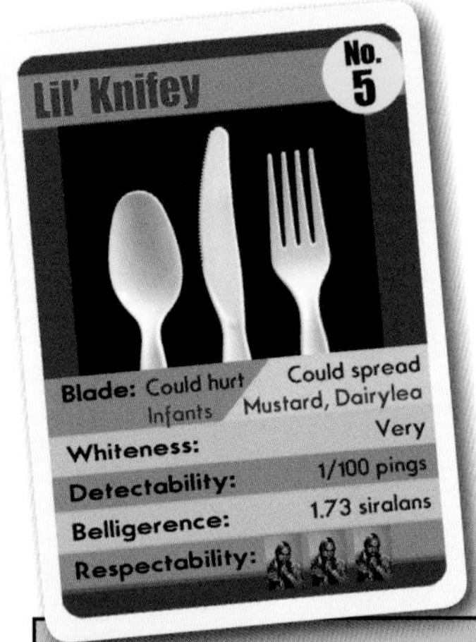

No. 5: Lil' Knifey

While it is not the sharpest of blades, Lil' Knifey's robust, serrated edge is capable of rendering victims badly grazed and really quite sore with sufficiently enthusiastic application. Often acquired as part of a set – also including a poking fork, a spoon, a packet of sugar and a moist towelette – this little fella is extremely popular with kids who are new to the knife-carrying circuit, and is almost impossible to detect. However, for all its dangers, most Lil' Knifey attacks can be easily deflected with a paper plate or some sufficiently leathery ham.

No. 11: Alan Titchmarsh's Trowel of Death

Particularly popular with the notorious GreenFingaz Massive, Alan Titchmarsh's initially welcome foray into blacksmithery sadly turned out to be just as proficient at weeding organs from perfect strangers as it was weeding the driveway. For months, the GFM, and sister group, the Deadly Hoes, have been terrorising allotments across the capital, but despite serious pressure from locals, and Alan himself, B&Q continues to stock and sell the range. Steer clear of anyone with muddy knees or wearing wellies.

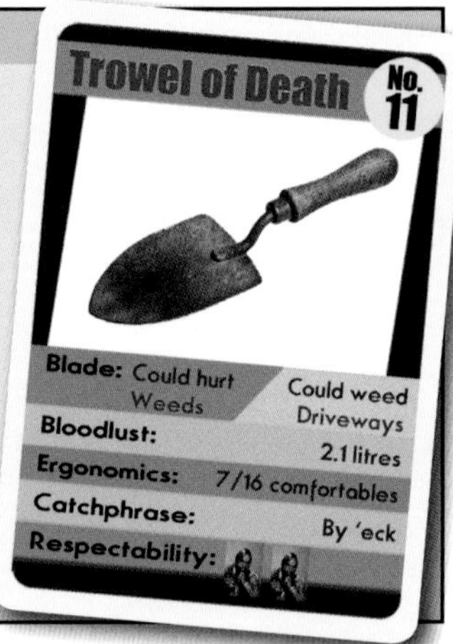

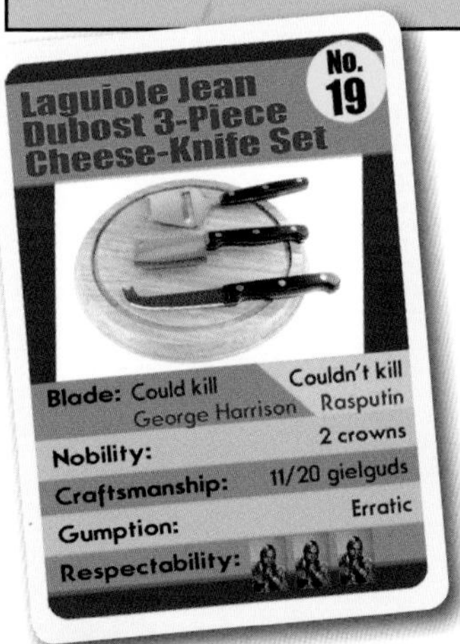

No. 19: Laguiole Jean Dubost 3-Piece Cheese-Knife Set

Hand-crafted in the Auvergne, the Jean Dubost range has now become an essential part of the more effete gangster's arsenal, and police believe was recently used to lethal effect by Rory 'Glugs' Shipton and the Murder-Rahs on a rather vicious raid at Henley Regatta that left three Pimms distributors needing medical care. Typical MO is to fell the target using the set's showpiece cheesy cleaver, then move in with the accompanying spreader and poker to finish the job.

No. 8: Excalibur

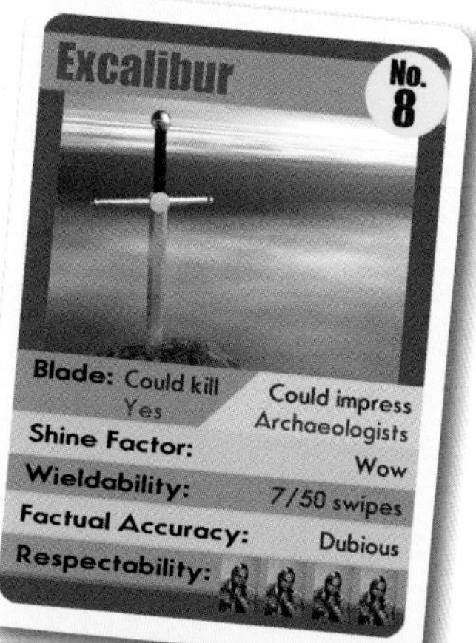

The popularity of broadswords on London's streets hit a peak during the first series of BBC One's 'Merlin'only to be superceded as the capital's weapon of choice by the decorative skates of 'Dancing On Ice'. Still, the idea of mighty Excalibur can't help but strike the fear of God into most of us, but given its extraordinary weight and the shameful puniness of modern youth, will probably never play more than a symbolic role amongst the capital's gangs. Some say it is just a myth, while others say it lies at the bottom of a reservoir in Staines, waiting to be reclaimed by the one true king of the streets.

Knife 4 Life
No. 14
Blade: Could hurt Sainsbury's
Could save Planet Earth
Fibre: 17% RDA
Fragrance: Pine Fresh
Social Responsibilty: Lovely
Respectability:

No. 14: Tesco's Knife 4 Life

Organic, biodegradable and, sadly, totally lethal, Tesco's Knife 4 Life is a classic example of an admirable concept poisoned by street crime. Aimed at keeping middle-class housewives' consciences clear while they julienned the butternut squash, the Knife 4 Life instead allows any hoodlum (or hoodla) to pay a £5 deposit and be armed ad infinitum, as Tesco will replenish each blade after use. To appease public anger, Tesco have launched Whittle 4 Life, a mass-production woodwork programme for young offenders and immigrants.

No. 39: Skywalker's Revenge

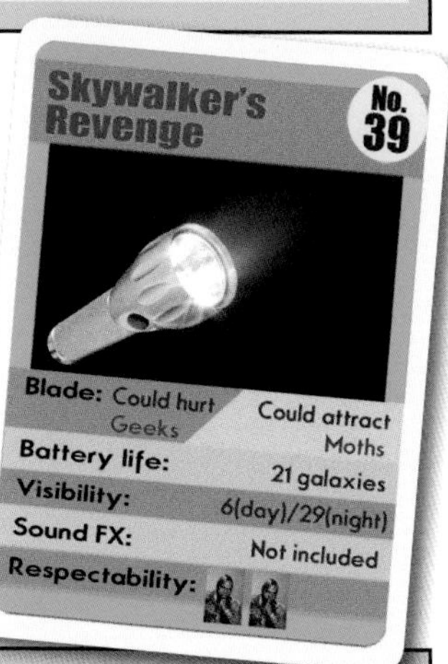

Although these 'weapons' pose abolutely no danger, anyone wielding one should be treated with extreme caution as they are guaranteed to be more than a little bit mental. Generally proceeded by an irritating, buzzing, swooshy noise, a blow from one of these can, in extreme cases, cause mild blindness, although most victims have reported symptoms ranging from 'temporarily increased visibility' to 'everything being a little bit brighter'. If you are threatened with an attack run away, or wait for the batteries to run out.

No. 34: The Pike

Only one gang in London is known to carry The Pike because no one else wears big enough trousers. First adopted as a stop-gap when someone's remote control fell in their tea and never recovered, The Pike soon became popular out and about due to the fact it could be easily excused as part of a school history assignment on the Plantagenets. If attacked, try to push your assailant for details of Edward I's reign, they may well find this distressing. However, try to avoid mentioning Edward II if at all possible. Just in case.

GET IT OFF YOUR TEXT...

Mobile moans from commuter drones

How come we can get a man on the moon and yet we havnt managed to prevent credit card fraud?

Ralph, Sutton

Does anyone else think Osama Bin Laden has modelled himself on Jafar from Aladdin?

Zander, Pimlico

As I read about rich celebrities, Im sitting opposite a homeless begging for a sandwich. Fair?

Caro, Camden

If children wore muzzles we wouldn't have the same problems with teenage gangs and stabbings that we have now.

Richard, St Johns Wood

To those who defend the Third World: why is my rice so bland?

Bernard, Balham

Re: thursday's chatz abt genocide – I completely agree, it mustn't happen again.

Tibs, Richmond

Has anyone actually seen any members of the so-called 'Labour' party getting their hands dirty on a building site or at a quarry? Thought not.

Fiona, Maida Vale

THE MINI-TERVIEWS

6 seconds with Robert Mugabe

LS: So, Robert, why do you keep coming back to London and what do you like about it?

RM: I come to crush the imperialist hand of....

LS: Great! What do you think of Lily Allen? Should she have stuck to her singing career or is she fresh and zany on TV?

RM: Listen, do not talk to me about a humanitarian crisis, the British Empire brought...

LS: Yeah. Who's your favourite T4 presenter?

RM: Hyperinflation is not my....

LS: Cheers Rob, that's all we've got time for. Love you!

4 secs Miquita Oliver

LS: How would you describe yourself in a word?

MO: Blessed.

LS: Do you like houmous?

MO: Only on pitta.

LS: Have you seen Gladiator?

MO: Yes, I have it on DVD.

LS: Where's the UN going wrong?

MO: Bureaucracy – an overwrought administrative structure.

2s w/John Sargeant

LS: So, you've seen it all from covering the IRA to jousting with Mrs Thatcher and then living the dream on the dancefloor. Was it all really great?

JS: Yes. Really great.

1" + Douglas Hurd

LS: Puppies or Kittens?

DH: Puppies, definitely.

DOMESTIC SLAVE OF THE DAY

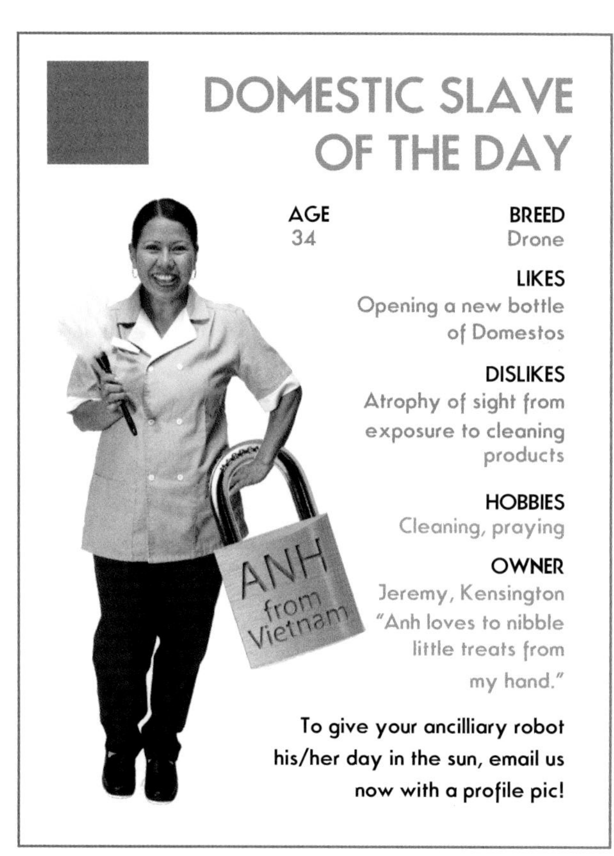

AGE
34

BREED
Drone

LIKES
Opening a new bottle of Domestos

DISLIKES
Atrophy of sight from exposure to cleaning products

HOBBIES
Cleaning, praying

OWNER
Jeremy, Kensington
"Anh loves to nibble little treats from my hand."

To give your ancilliary robot his/her day in the sun, email us now with a profile pic!

Thinking for London

If we all just focus on the little things...

...we can make a really big difference.

I ONLY KNOW THIS MUCH...

The Gift Of Celebrity Wisdom

Shrivelled knowledge fruit from SEAN CONNERY

Jesus was a Scotsman
He was born near Dumfries but tired of English rule so moved to the Holy Land where he started doing all his fancy stuff.

The best part of making love is just after the beginning
It gets really boring after that.

No animal can run faster than me
A cheetah came close once but that was it.

There's too much war
But there's nothing I can do about it. I've tried, but they just won't return my phonecalls.

Roger Moore doesn't like being called 'Moore'
But I do it anyway.

There's no business like show business
Is the saying.

I can't stand creme fraiche
It's just one of those things.

Introducing... PLANKTON

L-S introduces you to Plankton, London's noisiest visual thinker, putting the spunk back into political "cartoons"...

Stare, think, believe, action.

TOO MANY CHEFS SPOIL THE BROWN

a Plankton canvas

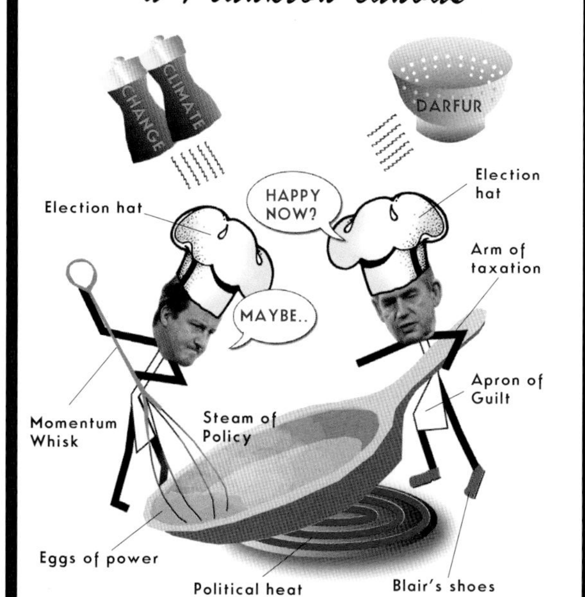

How We Be

"Be all you can be!" – but what if you really can't be more than you are?

FOLLOW OUR GIFT METHODOLOGY FOR ACHIEVING TOTAL SPIRITUAL BOUNDARYLESSNESS AND GAIN THE CONFIDENCE TO FIGHT ANOTHER DAY!

GET COMFY – If the Buddha could attain enlightenment through discomfort, just imagine how much happier he would have been if he'd done the whole thing sitting on a comfy bean bag. It just makes sense!

INTERFERE – The key to feeling great is confidence. Elbowing your way into other people's problems will make you feel assertive and will do wonders for your self esteem.

FANTASISE – The likelihood is your own life will have some massive problems that no one can fix, least of all you. Get away from it all by grabbing a flashy mag or going to the cinema and imagining you're someone else. Just shut your eyes and you're there! Good for stopping you from crying.

TURKEY – is a really great destination for a mini break or the full two weeks. Cleaner than you'd think and very well priced. You'll come back reinvigorated.

That's The ShitE-tiquette!

Ever accidentally stolen a pen, impulse-bought a pellet gun or punched a bishop? Nightmare! London Shite's Etiquette Panel are here to make sure our readers can make the right choices...

MEET THE PANEL

JIXY MCMAHON:
UK's leading etiquette and better-choice adviser.
www.jixymcmahon.com

DR BASTION SYNGE:
London Shite's sex guru. He is a doctor and has been on television.

STEVE DUXBURY:
Director of Postgraduate Studies in Decisions at the University of Keele.

NIGHTMARE ONE

"After my husband suggested we spice up our sex-life he brought a 17-year-old Filipino boy to our timeshare in the Algarve. It was certainly jazzy to begin with but he's now living in our house and a signatory on our joint account? Is this still sexy? Am I moving towards Carrie from SATC or away?"

"Empower yourself with an assertiveness course."

Jixt McMahon

"I think drastic action needs to be taken in one direction of your choosing."

Dr Bastion Synge

"Try 'Puerillians' – the Roman act of dressing up as a boy and speaking in a high-pitched voice."

Steve Duxbury

NIGHTMARE TWO

"I was introduced to the entire staff of the stationery firm I work at as 'Malcolm' on the first day I got here by an incompetent HR manager who has subsequently moved on. That was 14 years ago. My real name is Duncan. Is it too late to tell people or do I have to sit tight now?"

"Names are what we call each other in most global cultures so therefore have very high soul-importance. Arise Sir Duncan!"

Jixy McMahon

"Next time you trip over your laces or get pen on your face, ask yourself if Duncan would have done that."

Dr Bastion Synge

"Why not think of yourself as a less ambitious version of Batman/Bruce Wayne?"

Steve Duxbury

NIGHTMARE THREE

"I had a bit of a tiff with one of my best girlfriends last week when we went out for a mate's birthday. She made a bitchy remark about my top so I waited until the others weren't looking and then punched her in the kidneys and threw her off a bridge. Will things go back to being normal next time we meet?"

"Sometimes violence is the most cathartic form of detoxing friendships. Most of the 'Weekend Getaways' that I run end in abject bloodshed."

Jixy McMahon

"Remember 'actions' can have dire consequences. Try to get revenge through words like 'whoremonger'."

Dr Bastion Synge

"This is terrific news – my in-laws and I have had a much clearer understanding ever since I shot their dog. Bravo!"

Steve Duxbury

Trim Your Bitz

Muffin tops? Butcher's elbows? Fat chin? Read our guide to your body and get in shape. DO IT NOW!

Lobus Flagillens ("Flappy Lobe")
A pert, toned face can be really let down by unattractive earlobes, and in the gym they can be a safety hazard. In your own time, hang a salami (about 500g) from each ear and perform 100 squats.

Cerebral Weft
The brow is one of the most commonly neglected muscle groups. Rest your forehead on an exercise ball, take your weight on your knees and clap for 5–10 minutes.

Pre-nodal Chords ("Gordon's Peninsula")
To tone up these pesky neck muscles, try to spend at least 20 mins a day furiously agreeing or disagreeing with someone.

John Leslie's Chasm
This needs to be toned rather than built up, to maintain a beautiful smooth passage. Poke the handle of a croquet mallet down there and try to balance it vertically for 5-7 minutes.

Trapezic Plinth
The Plinths are stimulated by regular, low-energy office admin. Stapling and filing twice a day can work wonders.

Wrists
The good thing about wrists is that you can excercise them anywhere. Just take a bum bag of dough whenever you step out and knead it periodically throughout the day. Even on the tube!

Major Plutoid
The second biggest muscle group after the tongue, you really need to work this big fella pretty hard to get results. Try hauling a fat man out of a bath a couple of evenings a week.

Minor Plutoid ("Anus")
Spend a few minutes each day doing something that is just too fast to be classified as walking, but isn't quite jogging yet to get this nicely firmed up.

Adenoidal Spaz
Dancing is a great, fun way of slimming down a flabby spaz. Something slow like The Verve is probably the most effective accompaniment.

WIN A LIFETIME'S FREE GYM MEMBERSHIP

We've teamed up with London's premier sweat-inducers, The Flesh Creche, to offer one lucky reader a lifetime membership, including...

FULL ACCESS TO ALL CORE WORKOUTS

Session	Leader	Level	Equipment	Soundtrack	Target
Body Twang	Darren	Any	BodyTwanger	Noise	Tune Up Latissimi Polyfili
Muscle Gush	Darren	Physically Inferior	Peccavit Liqui-Plugs	Darren Shouting	Get Less Inadequate
HokeyKoke Aerobix	Darren	Quite Puny	Hula Hoop	Belligerent Playground Trance	Release Inner Child, Strengthen Outer Adult
Saints and Thinners	Andrew	Self-Loathing	Prayer Cushion	Rosary Beats	Hope God Will Make You Less Hideous
Pecsavers	DArren	Essentially Worthless	Steroids	Darren Sobbing	Compensate For Past Failures

DISCOUNTS ON ADVANCED WORKOUTS LIKE ...

NEAR-TERMINAL VÉLO - CITY

If you're over 50 and out of shape but put off by 'loud' techno-cycling try this soothing workout on antique French bikes. With Tom-Tom guides to Europe's most beautiful capital cities projected onto the wall, you'll have the cycling holiday of a lifetime!

'Pedal with Ricky'

Enjoy a sensuous trip down the Loire with balding hearthrob Rick Stein. Pedal next to Stein's barge as it sails down this majestic river, stopping off at the food markets of Blois and Chinon. Scrummy!

GET IT OFF YOUR TEXT...

Mobile moans from commuter drones

Fur protestors, what hypocrites. If you were chased by a seal pup in the wild, you would be the first to club it to death and wear its skin as a waistcoat. Get over yourselves!

Antoinette, Chelsea

Priests: can I oversee a funeral in flip-flops? Any advice most welcome.

Stephen, Amersham

Does anyone know why Karl Lagerfeld always has that neck brace on? Is he just a terrible driver?

Olivia, Notting Hill

My tip for 2010? Tabards. Trust me, they're going to be big.

Wexy, Shoreditch

I'm starting a competitive new job next week. I want to show them I mean business, but I've never tried "power-dressing" before. Can I wear a crown and carry a sceptre? Or is that going too far? Anyone, help!!

Sarah, Southfields

Anyone know where John Nettles buys his shirts? They're really striking. Best dressed man on TV. Period.

Jez, Islington

Get The Look

Pushing the envelope as ever, our 'out-there' approach to everyday fashion consistently adds an exciting edge and real sense of drama to the London scene. This breakdown of cellar-based icon Joey Fritzl's retro vibe proved an instant classic.

Over My Dead... Face

Reinvigorate even the craggiest visage with our guide to the best anti-aging creams money can buy.

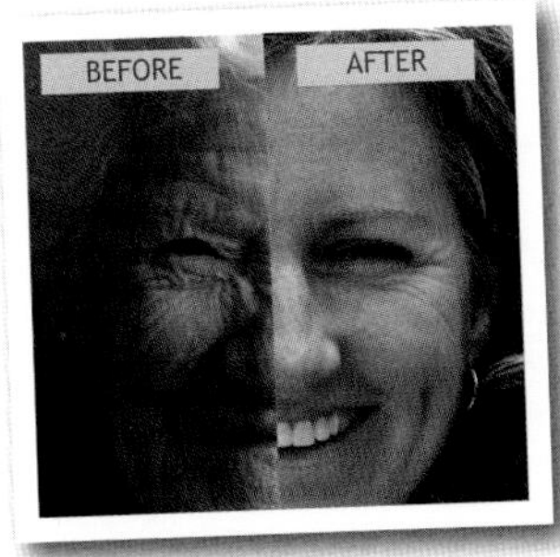

Body Shop Organic Spelt and Blessed Dew Nourishment Paste (inc. audiobook)

A 100% organic product that combines the life-giving wheatiness of spelt with the natural moisture of dew. The paste is made according to an old Druid recipe; Druids fed the mixture to their livestock on festival days. Each pot also comes with a willow swab for applying the paste, and a 60-minute audio CD of a Native American man saying kind words.

Success: 7/10. Not hugely effective, but the Native American sounds a bit like Pierce Brosnan. Dreamy!

Fructis "Skinfusions"

The newest addition to the Fructis "Skinimitable You" range, this is a great little creamy elixir with a double whammy. Skinfusions are more than just moisturisers - they work by causing large-scale water retention across the whole body, plumping out the skin and rendering wrinkles virtually invisible. And the bonus? No icky sweat patches! In a sample of 500 women, 80% of those that were able to speak after using the cream made a noise that sounded like they were either quite satisfied or very satisfied with the results.

Success: 8/10. If you can put up with the massive weight gain and loss of mobility, the results are incredible.

L'Oréal Maxi-10 Turbo Remoulding Serum

Originally developed by NASA during the Cold War in a bid to create a breed of super soldiers, this industrial strength rejuvenating serum has a delicious fragrance and a relatively short half-life to boot. Maxi-10 works through the same principles as Dr Gunther von Hagens "Bodyworlds" exhibition, by plasticizing any living tissue it comes into contact with. You'll need to apply it monthly to make sure those pesky cells don't make a comeback. The chunky lead-lined storage unit also has a kooky 1950s' charm - but you might need to get your boyfriend to lug it home for you!

Success: 9.5/10. Strong enough to reanimate Andie Macdowell's undead corpse.

Celebrity Smells

Get yourself your very own whiff of fame with London Shite's exclusive guide to the top five celebrity pongs.

THINK!

a pensive new fragrance from Brian Blessed

a clumsy new fragrance from Richard Hammond

HUSTLE

a no-nonsense fragrance from Paul Scholes

an unrelenting fragrance from Krishnan Guru Murthy

BLASPHIME

a heretical male fragrance from Rowan Williams

Ched Atkinson... VALUE PIMP

Is dignity getting in the way of a more economical lifestyle for you and your family? Money-saving guru Ched Atkinson thinks so and his remorseless search for value can change your life! Here are his Top Tips...

VOUCHER OF THE YEAR

Retailer: Better Days Funeral Services

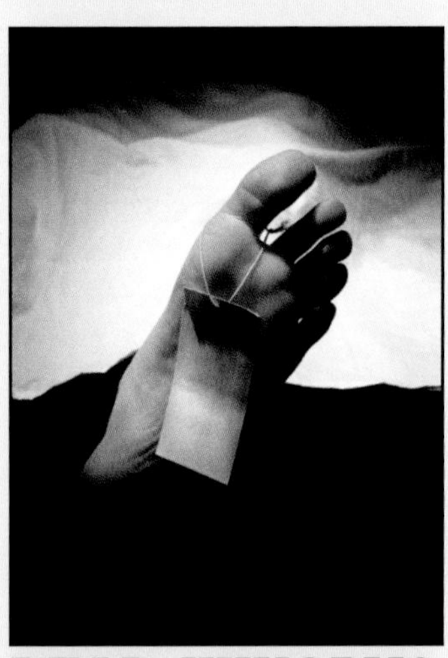

DEAD. HUNGRY?

With this exclusive offer available at all of our 200 nationwide outlets, you can get our Inferno cremation service free of charge when you book an adjacent 'Farewell Room' for the wake and order a Medium or Feasty Buffet.

TOP TIP 1

LOOK WHAT THE CAT DRAGGED IN...

Grumble: Most of my weekly shop is going on expensive and flashy "food" items – surely I can cut back?

Solution: Why spend your money on fancy staples like bread? Buy a tin of cat food at around 79p, scrape off the saline gel and nourish on the energy-yielding meat.

TOP TIP 2

THE GREAT TRAIN ROBBERY

Grumble: Train companies are killing me with their exorbitant prices – surely some kind of baseless attack on their staff could work?

Solution: Yes, you are exactly right. The prices we are expected to pay for "trains" that don't even fly in the air or go across water is scandalous. So when asked to cough up for this archaic form of transport, I employ a bargaining tactic I call "intimidation" to scare the train manager into submission. Try it by researching the intimate personal details of your local train managers then terrify them into letting you travel free of charge with threats involving their extended family and baseless allegations about their spouses (see above "template"). For lonelier train staff, Photoshop can be used to create visual evidence to "confirm" paedophilic or incestuous taunts. Remember, hate is free.

TOP TIP 3

TURNING IT INTO A BIG ISSUE

GRUMBLE: I'm working my socks off in a day job to pay my mortgage while the high street is full of smug homelesses making sweet cash selling their comic!

SOLUTION: Round up the *Big Issue* sellers in your local area and entice them with promises of sweets and heroin into working with you. Soon you will have the exploitative cartel you've always wanted and you'll be looking for a *second* home in no time.

TOP TIP 4

'HELLO MY NAME IS RAIN MAN - HOW CAN I HELP TODAY?'

GRUMBLE: When my shop is totted up at the till it's always more than I'd budgeted for. How can I shave a few pounds off?

SOLUTION: Your answer lies on the shop floor. Break and disfigure the most important items in your shop and blame it on the mentally "retarded" shelf-stacker these stores are forced to employ (there is always one). The store manger won't want to make a scene and you'll get that microwave you drew on with crayon for under a tenner.

BONUS TIP

FOR THE HARDCORE VALUE WHORE, WHY NOT JUST CUT OUT THIS MENDICANCY TEMPLATE AND HIT YOUR LOCAL TUBE STATION, MAJOR SUPERMARKET OR BUSY STRETCH OF PAVEMENT?

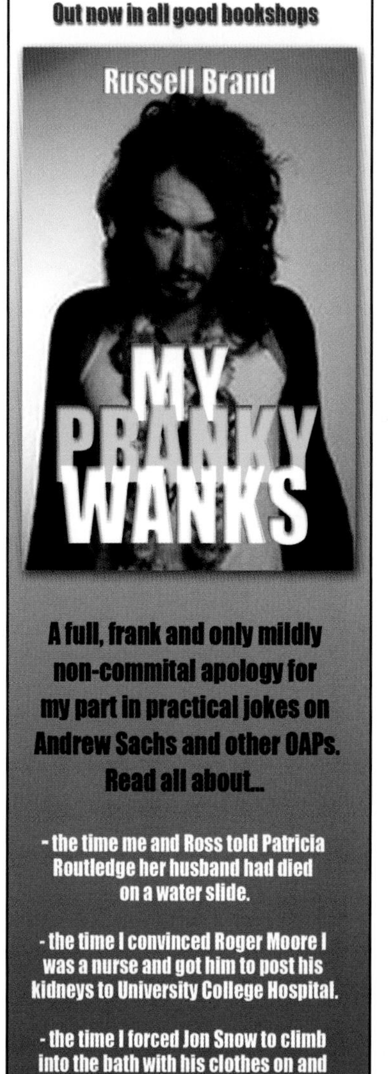

Be... GIRLIE

London Shite have teamed up with ayurvedic washing powder manufacturers Klëën and created a unique personality quiz to determine which product suits your clothes, and soul, best. Are you Precocious Saffron, Wafty Ocean Flavours or Dainty Sausage? Take the test and find out...

1. How would you describe yourself in a guttural noise?
A: Ahhhhhhsssppphhh...
B: Hefffllhhhh...
C: Ghewhindaaarss...

2. Which celeb is your style icon?
A: Helen Mirren
B: Judi Dench
C: Michael Gambon

3. If you lost your shoes, where is the first place you would look?
A: Go free and abandon your shoes.
B: Where you took them off.
C: Where you think they are.

4. It's a freezing cold night in West Riding, Yorkshire. The year is 1974 and the Yorkshire Ripper is on the rampage, yet to be caught. You are a prostitute. Do you...
A: Stay on the game. You need the cash.
B: Sleep in a wheelie bin and go to the Job Centre the next day.
C: Get flustered.

5: What's your ideal first date?
A: The new exhibition at the Tate, a glass of sherry, heavy petting and innuendo.
B: Cinema followed by disappointing tapas – you bond over the poor service prevalent in Spanish restaurants and then copulate furiously.
C: Cocktails and a chicken supreme at an Aberdeen Angus steakhouse.

6. What's your favourite charitable cause?
A: Previously unknown third-world instrumentalists or hard-up art critics.
B: Something quick and easy – RNIB probably.
C: One of the big hits – Iraq or Geldof related.

If you answered...

MOSTLY As: Your name is Suzi, you've recently divorced but you've found a spirit and youth you never knew you had. You enjoy long walks with your dog and salad-lunches with fatter, less happy friends. Please feel free to use any of our products - you are brilliant!

MOSTLY Bs: You are Angela, a 50-year-old solicitor in an atrophying marriage but with no time to sort it out. What with the kids disappearing into online gaming communities and soft drugs respectively you have no time to debate what detergent you use. Just grab Dainty Sausage and be done with it.

MOSTLY Cs: Well, hello Michaela. Thanks for your answers but you're not what we're looking for from a consumer. Please try the lower shelves.

Be... MANLY

Back in early 2009 we synergised with the Department of Health to create a groundbreaking depth-perception survey into the sex life of London's 'lad' population, and offer handy tips from experts on how it could be improved...

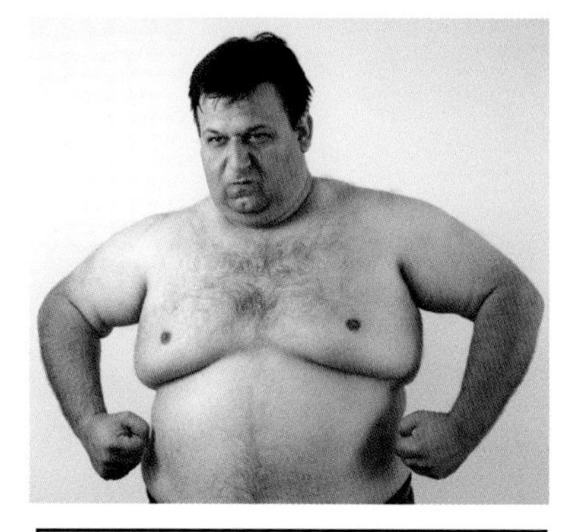

DR BASTION SYNGE'S TOP 5 SEX TIPS

STATS

37% of men have had the 'Helen Daniels' dream.

4.560 men have thought about the 'Wallace and Gromit' role-play

67% of men shout the phrase 'really great' during intercourse.

45gb the amount of unplayed music on men's iPods that resides in the 'Potential Sex' playlist.

1. Remember, penetrative sex does absolutely nothing for your female partner and can never possibly arouse her. To try and keep her interested, tell her about your day or a funny incident at the office as you work away 'downstairs'. This way at least, she won't lose interest all together.

2. If you suffer from a poor or tardy erection - don't worry it's perfectly normal! Just be sure to make a joke about it to break the tension. Try anthropomorphosizing your member as an indolent and work-shy labourer.

3. Always be polite and check before you make the next move towards a home run. Obviously run it past your partner first, but also make sure to ask the body-part in question as well. Although it can't actually respond, you will look far more chivalrous.

4. Thrusting away for hours on end doesn't make you a stud or a great sexual partner. It does, however, burn a lot of calories. If your partner is happy to be used as a body-gym then so much the better but do check.

TALKING HEAD
Vox Pops From Cock Jocks

"I thought about roleplaying with my girlfriend where she's a prostitute and I'm a sweaty punter but it was too much effort so I just got a hooker instead" *Phil*, 36, London

"I try to prolong sexual intercourse by thinking about my dead granny's funeral but sometimes I accidentally think about my other granny who's really fit and it's an absolute disaster!" *Peter*, 23, St Albans

"I'm pure sexual deviance and only get off on reworking biblical themes to spice up my wife and her boring fanny. Last night I was an angry Herod demanding retribution – naughty!" *Rowan*, 59, Canterbury

SOPHISTO-PORN

The *London Shite* DVD Club invites you under the covers with three of the most thought-provoking pornographs in recent years.

THE LIVES OF MOTHERS

Set in Stasi controlled East Germany, this harrowing yet smutty film focuses on three politically minded housewives who use their big fannies to get what they want.

CLOISTER FUCK

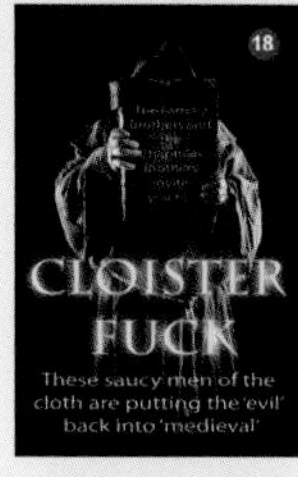

Written and performed entirely in ecclesiastical Latin, this is a story of lusty passion amongst the abbots and abbesses of a plague-ridden medieval community.

RESERVOIR DOGGINGS

Harmony Korine directs 8 bronzed gap-year students doing work-experience at Yarrow Reservoir in Rivington, Lancashire. Except the thing they get most experience of is uninhibited, gratuitious cock, fanny and balls. Heartbreaking.

The London Shite Guide to... Parties

It's Saturday night, you're in a loud bar or the flat of a colleague you dislike, your back aches from standing and you realize you don't like any of your friends... YOU'RE HAVING AN AWFUL TIME... but here's how to make sure it doesn't get any worse by ensuring you avoid the London party scene's most annoying but prevalant species of party-goer.

ENTRANCE

YOU FEEL A SWEATY PALM AROUND YOUR SHOULDER, IT'S THE...

UBIQUITOUS SCOTCH TWAT

Name: Malky

Do: Mention how Irvine Welsh is a modern day Yeats

Don't: Make a harmless remark about the pitfalls of substance abuse

Can be relied up to: Pronounce olives or anything above the foetid lifestyle he projects to be "too posh"

Cue to leave: "Yep, definitely Connery's the best... no, thanks I'm clean now plus I had a big dinner. Have a great night yeah?"

HEAD TO LIVING ROOM!

A KNEELING TWENTYSOMETHING IS BLOCKING YOUR ROUTE TO A CHAIR,IT MUST BE THE...

CROUCHING FANNY-CHASER

Name: Duncs

Do: Push tables near to sofas to prevent him from crouching into countless females throughout the evening

Don't: Ask him if he plays the guitar

Can be relied upon to: Gurn and say "as you do..." after everything you say

Cue to leave: "Tricky one but I'd probably still go for Parachutes over the recent one. Both great albums though. Just gonna get a drink, catch you later?"

LURK AT FRIDGE

A TRENDY FAT MAN IS DOLEFULLY LOOKING INTO THE MIDDLE DISTANCE, YOU'VE MET THE...

TUBBY BITTER GAY (TBG)

Name: Roy

Do: Show you're amused by, but don't smile at, an innuendo from his slutty harem of female friends

Don't: Ask him about his ill cat

Can be relied upon to: Roll his eyes impassively at everything that is said whilst tucking his belly back beneath his skin-tight T-shirt

Cue to leave: "Yeah, I suppose they can understand us but they just don't show it like humans do. Do you know where the toilet is?"

QUEUE FOR TOILET

YOU HAND IS CRUMPLED BY THE FIRM SHAKE OF...

THE SASS IN THE POWER SUIT

Name: Sara

Do: Agree that her son should be in a class above, his pasta collage of Dunkirk was sensational

Don't: Be frightened by her outsized lapels

Can be relied upon to: Demoralise

Cue to leave: "No that sounds like plenty of room for an au-pair. Yep, I'll just go in here now"

MOVE OUTSIDE

SOMEONE IS TALKING ABOUT HOW BRAVE HE HAS TO BE. IT'S...

THE UNSUCCESSFUL ACTOR/ WRITER/CREATIVE

Name: Keston

Do: Praise his hilarious performance as Falstaff at the open air Shakespeare festival

Don't: Praise his hilarious performance as "Man With Headache" in Holby City

Can be relied upon to: Wear a kooky, ethnic scarf that will draw attention away from the fact that he's wearing some sandals he found in a skip

Cue to leave: "You're probably right, the only way to really evoke the trauma of a rape is through dance... I'm going now."

TRY TO LEAVE

SOMEONE ADDRESSES YOU WITH ENTHUSIASM BUT GRAMMATICAL NEGLIGENCE. IT'S ONLY...

THE OPPRESSIVELY OVER-FRIENDLY EUROPEAN PROFESSIONAL

Name: Münt

Do: Agree with his assessment of the structural inadequacies of the rides at Alton Towers

Don't: Make offhand comments about "seeing him soon". He will honour the commitment

Can be relied upon to: Persistently attest to how much fun he's having, speaking directly into your ear until it is aching and spittle-flecked

Cue to leave: "The procedure for the drunken uninhibited sex? I think someone over there has the timetable. I'm going out for a cigarette."

PARTY-ING SHOT

Nip those awkward party-conversations in the bud with these cut-out-and-keep indicators.

The music is too loud and my ear hurts. I just want to eat some crisps and have a sit down.

I have a searing mouth ulcer and cannot speak to you. I hope you are well and your partner is also well. I haven't seen that film but I hope to soon.

BODY-TALK

Most experts now accept that 'body-language' is over 4 times more 'indicatory' than verbal communication. Here, our body-language expert shows us how to read the subtlest of symbols even in people no one cares about

NO. 1 STING AND TRUDI

Trudi's lack-lustre hair suggests miserly Sting won't even let his wife buy conditioner. By way of retaliation she has parted it on the left - Sting's least favourite side.

Sting has positioned himself in front of the frame of a painting to suggest that Trudi is "out of the picture".

Trudi looks more interested in the scotch eggs on the BAFTA buffet table than in her own husband.

Sting's disgust at his own wife has him behaving like some furious sea lion, literally roaring his disapproval.

Neither of Sting's hands are on his wife's breasts pointing to serious problems with intimacy.

The suit says: "I used to be in the Police", but the scarf says: "My wife won't touch my balls or shaft."

NO. 2 ROBERT AND CHARLES

A sullen, shame-faced expression and sagging shoulders suggests Prince Charles is in the dog house for something. Insensitive words over brunch? We think so.

It's all too much for the Sri Lankan Prime Minister, caught in this emotionally-charged cross-fire.

The Prince of Wales is head to toe in "white skin" while Bobby M has gone for a total "black" look, suggesting there is no coordination between the pair.

Robert's haughty brow seems to say: "The tiny denominations of your nations' currencies is laughable".

Without his usual flamboyant pocket handkerchief, Charles just isn't trying to impress Robert anymore.

Mugabe's positioning of a huge, blind mute between himself and Charlie surely points to a breakdown in communication.

Rob's insatiable lust has already picked out Princess Maria of Portugal as its next target.

ANOTHER GLOBE IMPROVING CAMPAIGN FROM LONDON SHITE

THE USB STICK CHALLENGE

CAN WE SEND 1 MILLION GIGABYTES TO THE THIRD WORLD?

COFFEE IS TRADED FAIRLY.
POVERTY IS HISTORY.
BUT...

IN SOME PARTS OF THE WORLD THE MOST NEEDY ARE STILL SURVIVING ON ARCHAIC FORMS OF DATA STORAGE

SEND IN YOUR UNWANTED USB STICKS TO US AND WE'LL GET TO HELPING PEOPLE LIKE...

SIMOK, A FARMER IN LAOS STILL ADMINISTERING HER PADDY FIELDS THROUGH FLOPPY DISCS

Dogging Direct.com

Same game. Different rules.

Why sit around in freezing parks or abandoned warehouses waiting for the perfect doggist to turn up?

Find your ideal partner at DoggingDirect.com

How We Ponder

INTRODUCING THE LONDON SHITE THINK TANK – WITH OVER 4 DIFFERENT TYPES OF CULTURE GOING ON IN LONDON ON ANY GIVEN NIGHT IT'S ALMOST IMPOSSIBLE FOR US TO KEEP UP WITH, CRITIQUE AND PILFER FROM ALL THE THINKY HAPPENINGS THAT ARE UNFOLDING.
HERE'S HOW WE ROLL...

LONDON SHITE'S THINK TANK

THINK (DON'T) – We adopt a 'jazz' method of finding our 'Critics Pick' venues. We feed the word 'culture' into the Think Tank's TomTom and end up at 10 uniquely varied but brilliant new cultural venues. Great for getting away from the 'popular' and the 'acclaimed'.

HEIGHTEN (AWARENESS) – AttentionPellets (the London Shite logo written in permanent marker) are fired against lesser-known fringe venues to try and drum up support for London's sub-culture from Joe Public.

INTERNET (BROWSE) – The web can throw up some zany clips with a 'quick-fun' rating that high culture just can't match.

NOVICES (SOURCE) – We thrive on finding the freshest, newest creators before anyone else. By scouring the city's most exclusive sixth-form colleges and monitoring the children of famous people, we find them first.

KARE ('CARE') – The Tank is then employed to help and cherish some of our more forgotten stars. We drop off a big shop to Richard Wilson and Michael Frayn and then Sean Bean is given a lift to his judo lesson.

Gadgets We Love...
THE CULTURE CADDY

"I really liked that Andy Warhol retrospective at the Tate. What did you think?"

Well? Too focussed on your career to worry yourself with actually thinking about things? Want to be culturally active without having to waste your time looking at paintings and listening to music? Want to have thoughts, but too tired to think of them yourself?

Then you need the CultureCaddy portable opinion interface. Using sentient digital culture nodes, this hand held device tells you exactly what to say about any current cultural event.

Your friend at work asks "What did you think of the Velazquez exhibition at the National Gallery?"

CultureCaddy says: "Moving and very expensive."

Your friend says "I can't believe Nigel was raving about that nude art installation."

CultureCaddy says: "I have grave doubts about Nigel as a human being and a father."

Your spouse asks: "Shall we go and see the new Swan Lake at Covent Garden?"

CultureCaddy says: "Yes. The music's phrasing is sublime and the facilities are hygienic."

Your wife says "I was surprised you didn't like the new Ian McEwan novel."

CultureCaddy says: "Maybe I'm not the person you married and if we can recognise that, then better for all."

Your father asks: "Did you catch the new Coen brothers' film?"

CultureCaddy says: "No, but his film make me many laugh."

3 settings:	Adequate, Ill-informed and Dunce
Choice of 3 voices:	Patrick Stewart, Germaine Greer or Bill Oddie
Choice of colour:	Pensive Tartan or Lobster Bisque
Plus... USB and mobile phone connectors allow CultureCaddy to respond automatically to emails, texts and phone calls	

THE KULTUREKADET

A handy nano-sized sentient advisor from the makers of The Culture Caddy designed to make sure your little poppet has the right answers for all those wrong questions!

Your son's friend says: 'Did you watch that pornography I sent you via the MySpace?'
KultureKadet tells your son to say: 'No, I get all the aesthetic beauty I need from Jules et Jim'

Your granddaughter's boyfriend says: 'Let's sneak into the National Gallery's special exhibit without paying!'
KultureKadet tells your granddaughter to say: 'Absolutely not. The British Arts' scene needs all the help it can get'

Your daughter's best friend says: 'Don't you think Judi Dench looks like Sooty?'
KultureKadet tells your daughter to say 'Dame Judi Dench is a national treasure and has done more for the thespian world than you will ever achieve.'

Top teen-celeb voices including Jamie Theakston, Terry Christian and Dani Behr

London Shite Launches Brand New SOBO Awards

London Shite is proud to announce the launch of our brand-new, all-encompassing, 'Stuff Of Black Origin' awards.

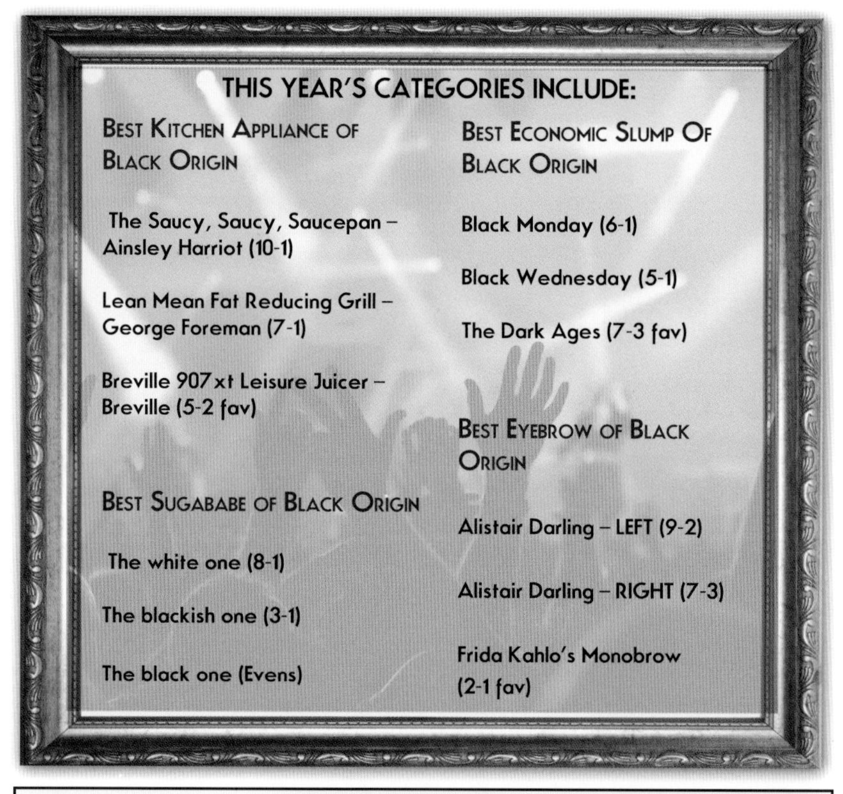

THIS YEAR'S CATEGORIES INCLUDE:

BEST KITCHEN APPLIANCE OF BLACK ORIGIN

The Saucy, Saucy, Saucepan – Ainsley Harriot (10-1)

Lean Mean Fat Reducing Grill – George Foreman (7-1)

Breville 907xt Leisure Juicer – Breville (5-2 fav)

BEST SUGABABE OF BLACK ORIGIN

The white one (8-1)

The blackish one (3-1)

The black one (Evens)

BEST ECONOMIC SLUMP OF BLACK ORIGIN

Black Monday (6-1)

Black Wednesday (5-1)

The Dark Ages (7-3 fav)

BEST EYEBROW OF BLACK ORIGIN

Alistair Darling – LEFT (9-2)

Alistair Darling – RIGHT (7-3)

Frida Kahlo's Monobrow (2-1 fav)

PLUS... WIN TICKETS TO THIS YEAR'S SHOW!

If you'd like to be in the audience for this magnificent occasion, you'll first need to check that you're OBO enough using our handy Sugababe OBO-meter (right). Then simply text 'I'm so OBO!' to 25225 and we'll put your name in the hat. Good luck!

LoveSalad HateNarrowmindedness

From the social pioneers who brought you the LoveMusic HateRacism festival, this year will see yet another deplorable trait banished from all our consciousnesses – this time through the medium of salad.

MAIN STAGE

VEGETABLE PUPPETRY DEMONSTRATIONS FROM JAMIE OLIVER (16:00-18:00)

HARD-FI PERFORMING 'THE HYMN OF HOMOGENOUS THOUGHT' - AN IRONIC MANTRA FOR THE WIDE OF MIND (18:30-19:00)

FLAGELLATION OF NON-ORGANIC FARMERS (19:00 'TIL LATE)

YAKULT STAGE

YOGHURT THERAPY SESSION (OVER 18S ONLY) (12:00-17:00)

LIVESTOCK GIVEAWAY (17:00-18:00)

"NARROW-MINDEDNESS FROM NINETIES TO NOUGHTIES" - POWERPOINT PRESENTATION BY RAZORLIGHT (19:00-19:15)

VEGETABLE INFO-TENT

MONTY DON'S INTERACTIVE LECTURE: "WHAT IS A LETTUCE, AND HOW DOES IT GROW?" (15:00-19:00)

KIDS' VEGETABLE COSTUME COMPETITION (16:00)

DOCUMENTARY: "THE HORRORS OF DARFUR" (16:30)

CHARLIE DIMMOCK MEMORIAL STAGE

EFFIGY OF ROBERT MUGABE TO BE PELTED WITH TUNA NICOISE THROUGHOUT THE DAY (12:00-CLOSING)

PLUS - Mind widening gift pack for every visitor

- Salad

WANT SOMETHING A LITTLE LESS WORTHY?

Check out this morally questionable festival from Britain's vibiest supermarkets....

For all those music fans burrowing haplessly below the poverty line, you can now catch this super festival, bringing together Britain's most adequate cover bands for a product-driven line-up based around the nation's favourite value products.

Unsatisfying but willing approximations of The Jam, Cream, Vanilla Ice, Korn, Salt 'n' Pepa and a selection of Tim Rice hits will be rocking out selected supermarket carparks for an astonishingly low entry fee of just 50p. Loyalty card holders get in free.

(Bring a pound for the trolleys.)

57th Annual London Shite Film Festival

THIS YEAR'S FESTIVAL LINE-UP WAS EASILY THE MOST CINEMATICALLY AMBITIOUS IN THE 57-YEAR HISTORY OF THIS WORLD-FAMOUS EVENT. WE PUSHED BOUNDARIES RIGHT TO THE LIMIT, AND THEN JUST STEPPED ON OVER TO THE OTHER SIDE AND PULLED THEM EVEN FURTHER INTO THE UNKNOWN. HERE, WE OFFER YOU AN EASILY ACCESSIBLE GUIDE TO THE BEST OF THE BEST.

BUFF BOOKS

Verbose and baffling male-grooming tips from Britain's favourite critic

Learn how to:

- Seduce like a fifties dandy
- Achieve sex through lurid cultural discourse
- Jive

THE MAN FROM DEL MONTE

dir: Paul Thomas Anderson

Multi-oscar winner Daniel Day-Lewis again deploys his infamous dedication to method acting to good effect in this stark portrayal of the violent rise to power of the eponymous juice magnate. Insiders have claimed the actor's dressing room was decorated like a giant fruit bowl where Day-Lewis would retire to spoon an 8ft-banana between takes, refusing to return to the set until he was 'ripe'.

THE CHAIR

dir: Alejandro Iñárritu

In his follow up to 2006's *Babel*, Iñárritu again deftly weaves seemingly unconnected and uninspiring story fragments into what appears to be a wildy incoherent mass, until suddenly, in a masterful twist, it is revealed that all the film's main characters had, at different times, sat down in the same chair.

BARTON: A 21st-CENTURY PORTRAIT

dir: Guy Ritchie

Part documentary, part installation art, this incredibly intimate film trains over 20 cameras on Britain's most enigmatic player - Joey Barton - as he sweats, grunts and swears his way through 90 mins of Newscastle Utd's torrid 2-2 away draw at West Ham last April. While essentially commentary free, except from a few thought provokingly racist subtitles, any whiff of pretention is emphatically crushed by Hard-Fi's epically abrasive soundtrack and director Guy Ritchie's street-savvy mis-en-scène, leaving behind a cinematic residue that is at once a grittily real depiction of sporting endeavour and a hauntingly beautiful portrait of a man.

MOYLES/PINOCHET

dir: Ron Howard

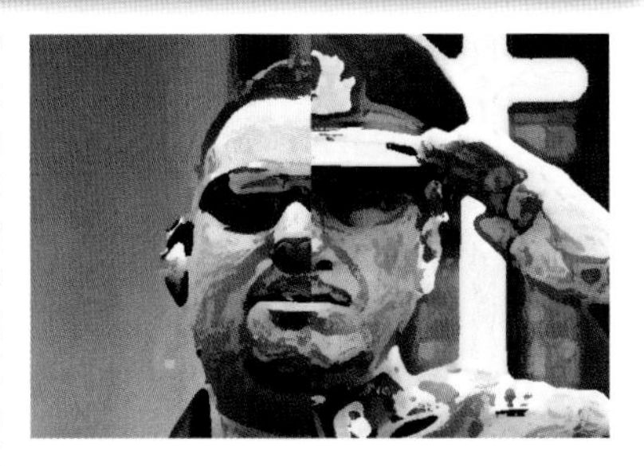

Originally starting out as a hit on the London stage, this electrifying account of the historic interview between murderous Chilean dictator, Augusto Pinochet, and Radio One's talking scrotum, Chris Moyles, finally gets the big screen treatment it deserves. Having been pardoned prosecution by the UK government, Pinochet chose Moyles to be his interrogator in a televised farewell interview, thinking, like many, that conversation would be limited to the benefits of urinating sitting down. Moyles, however, had other ideas, and deployed a combination of Sugababes records and repetitive burping to extract the full grisly confession that had previously eluded the legal might of at least three sovereign nations. Michael Sheen approaches the role of Moyles with considerable refinement, while Frank Langella impresses as the incontinent mass-murderer.

LITTLE BIG HORN

dir: Woody Allen

Woody Allen's latest genre-hop sees him step in front of the camera to take on the seedy world of pornography with a dollop of art-house sauce. He plays the chief protagonist, a 70-year-old man named 'Woody Allen', who for unexplained reasons becomes the world's most famous porn star and indulges in gratuitous sexual fantasies with the young and the nubile.

MY WIFE'S FACE

dir: Sam Mendes

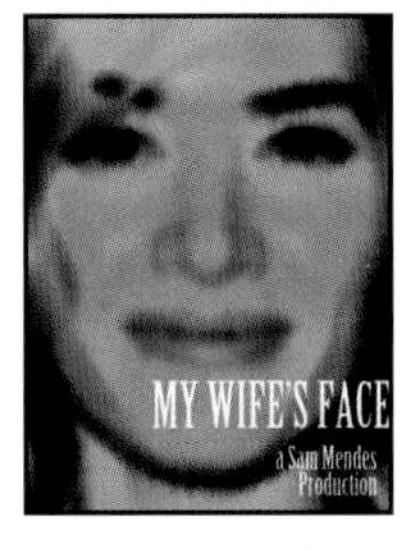

A 90-minute shot of Kate Winslet looking into camera and contorting herself through a range of emotions might sound like a tricky watch but you won't find anyone betting against it for the 'Best Actress' award across the board. Watch out for her brave 'spazz gurn' 33 minutes in.

WALK AWAY IN SILENCE

dir: Anthony Corbijn

From the producers of *Mamma Mia* comes a pared-down pop-romp based around the songs of Joy Division. Set in 1970s' Stockport, shy and dyslexic teen Norman is shocked when his mother tells him his father could be any of three men: his abusive step-father, a convicted rapist or Nobby Stiles. His slow mental and physical disintegration is peppered with all your favourite Ian Curtis hits.

HOXTON'S ALT FILM FESTIVAL

My Big Fat Greek Abortion

Greek cinema finally gets the place it deserves in the European canon with this haunting tale of unwanted babies.

The Colours of Nothing

Shot entirely in grey monochrome, this uncomfortable debut from Gregor Fuchaowski won the Golden Orb at Copenhagen this year. Filmed in the dead of night near the director's home town of Gillingham.

Nice Occasion

This Japanese romantic comedy is as utterly baffling as it is charming. It charts the story of a farm boy who falls in love with an orb of energy that can talk to plants.

L'Homme Qui Ne Dit Rien, Mais Quand Il Dit Quelque Chose, C'est Assez Bizarre

French veteran, Gérard Blagnac, who famously refuses to speak to any of the actors working for him, weaves another giddy spell here.

Le Nozze di Michele e Laura

This enchanting film was actually the wedding video recorded by Michele De Santis' father Cesare at his son's wedding in Naples last year. Having accidentally followed the trademark style of the Dogme movement, De Santis' home vid has become the toast of Europe.

THE HI-BROW LO-DOWN

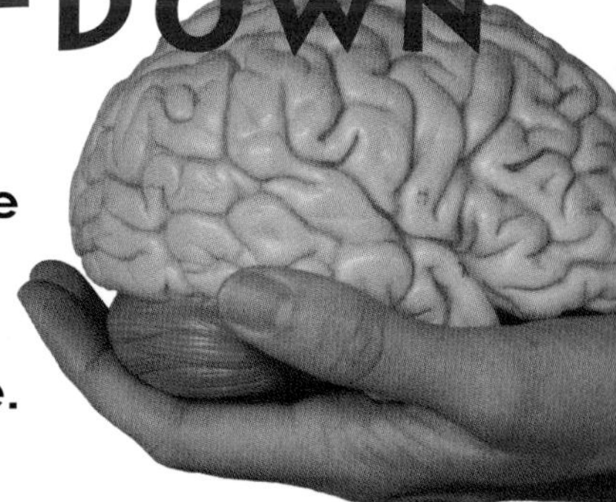

With yet another action-packed year ahead for hi-brow London happenings, it can be difficult to decide which one will make you do the most thoughts. This informative but poorly researched guide should help you get to the proverbial cultural honey-pot just fine.

50 CENT SAYS

VISIT THE BRITISH MUSEUM

"GET INFORMED ABOUT COLONIALISM OR DIE TRYIN'"

KILLER LOOKS @ THE V&A

Combining the social intrigue of homicidal maniacs with the aesthetic delight of pretty clothes, this thoughtful exhibition brings together the wardrobes of some of the world's most brutal and prolific killers. Coupled with grisly artefacts and harrowing pictures of their hapless victims, Killer Looks works its way through centuries of murderous garments - from the testosterone buffed armour of the Conquistadors to the sassy suits of Myra Hindley - to create one of the most inspiring exhibitions of the year.

From the gift shop: Half of London will probably soon be bedding down in the super comfy Pol Pot pyjama range, while Idi Amin's golf shoes should give you an indimidatory edge next time you play the boss.

REALLY BIG STUFF @ THE TATE MODERN

No artist better develops a theme and no artist better exploits a space than Louise Bourgeouis, and with Really Big Stuff at the Tate Modern, she's truly in her element. Cramming the Turbine Hall with totally humongous versions of everyday objects most of us would merely 'use', Bourgeois's work then bursts out onto the Southbank, challenging traditional dimensional thought with the terrifyingly huge 'French Fries' and converting the Tate's mighty chimney into a 76-ft tampon - all with devastating effect.

From the gift shop: They have a cool range of the really big stuff but shrunk back down to normal size again, including: The Really Small Big Raisin (£30), The Really Small Big Pencil (£40) and the soon-to-be-iconic Really Small Big 50 Pence Piece (£70).

HAROLD PINTER'S FREEZER @ THE HAYWARD GALLERY

For many, when the great playwright died last year, he was still just as enigmatic as when he first burst onto the scene back in the early Sixties. We may know his plays back to front, but how many of us really know Pinter: The Man? This haunting exhibition offers a rare insight into a literary great through a methodical investigation of what was left behind in his freezer - including some less-than-edible surprises.

From the gift shop: It's not often you get the chance to buy an exact replica of something a Nobel Prize winner has owned, but with Bird's Eye Fish FIngers available for just £22.50, it's hard to resist owning a little piece of history.

KA-BLAMMO! @ THE IMPERIAL WAR MUSEUM

For anyone that loves war, but gets a little sleepy being bogged down by unneccessary 'history', the Imperial War Museum's latest exhibition should be just the tonic. Co-curated by Jeremy Clarkson and Ross Kemp, KA-BLAMMO! reviews and recreates key explosions from the past and you can even help the boys reconstruct a working model of the world's first atomic bomb, 'Little Boy', to be redeployed in the New Year.

From the gift shop: Modelled around Sarah Connor's secret bunker from Terminator 2, you can essentially get your hands on anything that might go BANG!, from pre-inflated packets of crisps to pre-packed '7/7' rucksacks.

DINOSAURS DO THE FUNNIEST THINGS @ THE NATURAL HISTORY MUSEUM

After a particularly wild party for the Jurassic Department's 20,000,000 anniversary, staff at the Natural History museum awoke to find that they had drunkenly rearranged most of the museum's fossils into 'hilarious' poses, many involving traffic cones. With only 5 mins to opening time, they had no choice but to let the punters in, but the impromptu revamp was such a success it is still going to this day.

From the gift shop: Road safety equipment is now outselling dinosaur merchandise 3:1, but to fight back, the store is offering a free Pterydactyl skeleton with every 'Men At Work' sign purchased.

GET IT OFF YOUR TEXT...

Ill-informed opinion about something you don't understand? We love hearing about it...

Anyone else fed up of waiting when the red man flashes and crossing when the green man flashes? I'm fed up of this "government" telling us what to do.

Tony, NW3

The Olympics is a waste of money the money cd be spent better eg. on shorts for old ppl

Ranulph, W4

Peter (Txts, Jan 28th): You're right, the Ovidian hexameter is completely overwrought. Glad someone thinks the same!

Gemma, SW4

I dunno why everyone still watches Nigella Lawson wile there is a war going on in Afghanistan.

Greg, E5

Just been sick in a pram!!! Lol!!

"Treats", E1

I think it's about time this country said a firm "no" to Terence Stamp. He causes us nothing but trouble.

Breft, W5

Will someone please tell me I'm brilliant? And don't forget to watch the X-Factor ;-)

Dermot, W1

THIS IS LONDON DOUBLE AWARD WINNER
Most Pensive Arts Complex + Most Eclectic Snack Bar

Centrismo
Something thoughty...™

The Centrismo Culture Park's

Spring Timetable

From The Cafeteria

THE THOUGHTIEST DISHES IN LONDON

"DALI-CIOUS" SAMPLER MENU

Still running after last season's surrealism exhibition, choose from a range of bizarre but tasty dishes including a penis-shaped terrine, steamed trout balanced on a hammer, and a sponge pudding in a bowler hat.

FRANCIS BACON SANDWICH

A novel take on an English classic, this thought-provoking sarnie recreates the painter's disturbing depictions of the human form with skilfully arranged rashers of bacon and violent squirts of ketchup.

WAGNER BURGER

Delivered to your table to the rousing strains of Ride of the Valkyries, this elaborate 14-lb burger has all the grandeur of the composer himself. Finish it and get a free opera CD!

THE NAMESAKE LECTURES

BURRELL DOES BORRELL

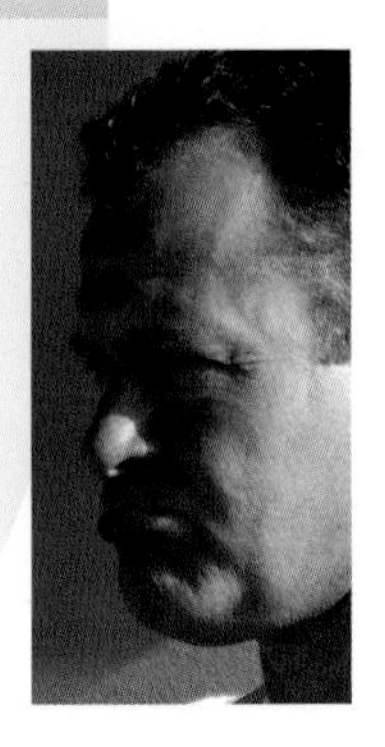

A night of budget entertainment as desperate but cheery ex-dogsbody Paul Burrell performs a selection of hits from Razorlight's back catalogue, accompanied by his wife on a drum.

Paul has also promised to mingle with audience members and perform card tricks and basic gymnastics during the interval.

GAZZA DOES GAZA

Confused ex-footballer Dr Paul Gascoigne talks for an indeterminate amount of time about the Middle East peace process and how he would solve it using his own unique brand of abrasive Geordie diplomacy.

With frequent digressions to tackle topics as diverse as the European Union, how to make a hat out of napkin, and why gypsies were responsible for Gazza's downfall, it promises to be an enthralling evening. No refunds.

KAYE KAYE KAYE DOES THE KKK

T4's toothiest regional personality Vernon Kaye gets to grips with the Ku Klux Klan, with an indepth discussion of the group's inception, development and role in the US Civil Rights Movement.

While the topic is a serious one, the irrepressible Kaye bounds through tales of lynching and race hate with wonderful enthusiasm, culminating in a duet with Tess Daly as Martin Luther King.

EXHIBITIONS

Burt Reynolds: My Eyebrows 1960-1979

A celebration of the actor's lesser known pieces of facial hair, and the various transformations they underwent between his appearances in "Perry Mason" (season 5 episode 27) and "Smokey and the Bandit".

Features an interactive eyebrow simulator.

MUSIC

Carlos Santana – The Dialysis Tour

The undisputed master of the soft porn soundtrack plays a selection of smooth guitar hits, interspersed with short spoken pieces to raise awareness of the perils of gall stones and kidney dysfunction among old people.

PLUS... THE LONDON JAZZ FESTIVAL

Jools Holland – Now That's What I Call Music 1-40

The awkward pianist plays the first of 2 "pop revisionist" gigs, ruining classic hits from the 80s and 90s by playing the same boogie-woogie piano riff over the top of them irrespective of their style or genre.

Carlton "Carlton Peterson" Peterson III

A solo sax master class from a veteran of the jazz scene. The only horn player to master the near impossible talent of playing hard bebop saxophone while simultaneously singing every word perfectly through his nose.

The Naughty Sounds Collective

More impenetrable noise from this 25-piece, who bill themselves as a mixture of acid jazz, post-colonial soul and ironic ambient harmonics. Look out for the surprisingly moving solo by the Hotpoint SDW60P dishwasher containing a tambourine.

Jazz 'n' Dave

The loveable cockney pair are back, blending cerebral, avant-garde jazz with their traditional pub sing-alongs. Expect hits from "Don't Give a Monkey's" and "Mustn't Grumble" spiced up with augmented 9th chords and extended synthesiser solos.

come, play KAMIKETTO adventurous number shape

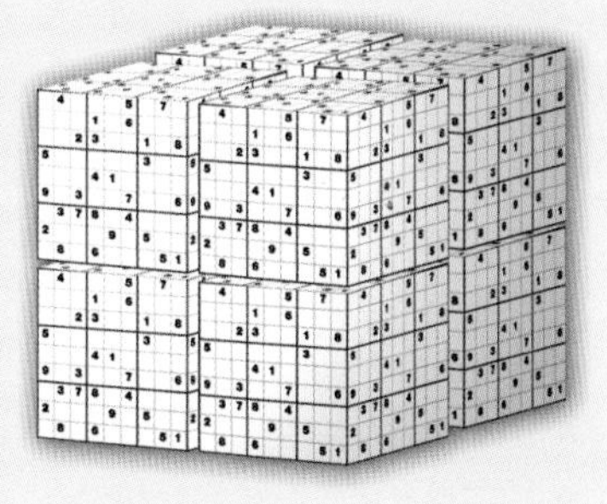

- start in the easiest top left cuboid (the 'Nancy Box') using a 2B pencil to fill in the absent numbers in each number-thimble.

- take the third prime of each number in that cuboid and fill out the bottom-right cuboid accordingly.

- in the top-line of the top-right cuboid, write your favourite number six times with a softer pencil before entirely replicating your favourite 4 lines from the two left-hand columns.

- now you're set for the 'Test of Sampson' in the bottom right corner where 1 number is given to you and 8 spaces need to be filled with the shapes or emotions you think symbolise that number best.

- take a step back and look at your cuboid-matrix - if it looks like an ox, you've got it! If it looks like a hawk, try again!

Fed up of all the music awards going to bands that people have heard of and enjoy listening to? Amen to that. Now that Mercury has done a Phil Collins on us, the Thallium Prize is now the number one UK award for celebrating genuinely progressive music and talented noisiness.

THE NOIZE CATEGORIES

Best Noises (Musical)

Best Noises (Non-musical)

Least Heard Of

Most Prolonged Song

Most Re-appraised

Most Spittle Expelled (Live Act Award)

Most Idiosyncratic Hat Wearer

Best Accompaniment to a Channel 4 Documentary

The Mark Ronson Special Award for Best Use of Trombone

CELEB GOODIE-BAGS

Nobody goes home empty-handed, or empty-hearted, as event organisers give all nominees an exclusive goodie-bag containing ethical, thought-provoking and delicious items worth well over £100.

EACH BAG INCLUDES:

- Sony Discman
- Jar of organic apricot jam
- Handwritten encouraging remarks from Stephen Fry
- One of Yoko Ono's teeth
- An ironic copy of Coldplay's first album
- Photo and adoption details of an impoverished child
- Cadbury's Heroes

ARTIST: THE MICK FORBES TRIO
ALBUM: Official Soundtrack to Hetty Wainthrop Investigates (Season 2)

Mick Forbes Trio

DEAL (WHAT IS IT WITH IT): With Forbes on synth and the brothers Jeff and Nigel Dorigo on bass and keys respectively, the trio recorded accompanying music for this Patricia Routledge-driven BBC smash back in 1997. The stand out track 'Hetty Smells A Rat' has already been sampled by PJ Harvey.

WHAT THE CRITICS SAY: "Forbes is playful, burnished and unflappable" Jess Huffing, Observer

ARTIST: DAVID ABLETT
ALBUM: Ablett Music #4

David Ablett

DEAL (WHAT IS IT WITH IT): Ablett, a retiring IT engineer, shot to fame last year when his bedroom-based Amstrad ramblings became the cherished plaything of 6music zeitgeist-bender, Steve Lamacq.

WHAT THE CRITICS SAY: 87% of T4 audiences pushed the red button symbolizing "Yes" when asked if this record was more seminal than their English GCSE coursework.

ARTIST: FUNTY
ALBUM: Ooh, I really like it!

Funty

DEAL (WHAT IS IT WITH IT): Hailed by the *Observer Music Monthly* as the "death knell for sophisto-pop", Funty are a five-piece slice of unreconstructed pop joy. With a glorious disregard for trends, their high energy, "Steps"-heavy debut will definitely make you do a smile.

WHAT THE CRITICS SAY: "Funty are to modern culture what Durer was to the Renaissance" Tom Paulin

ARTIST: SCREAMY BRIAN
ALBUM: Gonna Get Me A Brand New Hat

Screamy Brian

DEAL (WHAT IS IT WITH IT): One of the most honest singer/songwriters in recent years, Brian's unique brand of shoeless, urine-soaked blues has brought a fresh gust to the UK indie scene. This concept album charts 8 hours of the singer's life as he struggles to fashion a hat out of a newspaper, and was recorded in its entirety in the fire escape of a Nando's restaurant.

WHAT THE CRITICS SAY: "Beyond the aural panoply of his performances, there is the visceral force of his appalling body odour. Hit with that smell, one is forced to face terrible truths. 'Yes', one thinks, 'I am human'". David St John Grifty, Rolling Stone Magazine

Club Your Tits Off

Still hungry for culture long after the British Museum has switched off the lights? Luckily 'culture' is not just the realm of 'professors' and 'artists' - it's also obtainable through drugs and excessive sweating. Here's a peek into 'Clubland'...

Clubber's Club 2010

NAME: GANYMEDE'S PANTRY

What vibe?: Part cheez club part orgy-based fantasy-suite in an abandoned B&Q off the Holloway Road this is essentially a big sex shop but with loose normals offering themselves rather than fully certified prostitutes.

Why go?: Next time you get bored of clubbing amongst asinine simpletons with Ted Baker shirts and a Carphone Warehouse fringe, come and taste Ganymede's intoxicating nectar.

Wear what?: Silk Thai boxer shorts, a tie, but no shirt.

Man About Town

THE HOTTEST MOVER, SHAKER AND TINY TROUSER-WEARER ON THE LONDON CLUB SCENE

Clubbing name: D Moz
Real Name: Derek Moss, from Amersham
Plates spun: Producer, DJ, designer, organic farmer – pretty much the most talked about multi-creative in London.
History: With a career in IT support firmly behind him, he has become notorious for his pioneering DJ sets that incorporate a variety of music and sounds from the Beach Boys to whale song to the early internet dial-up tone.
Signature night: "Beat Abattoir", Sunday nights, 93 Feet East, Brick Lane (vegans get in free).
Also look out for: His delicious courgette ragout.

I Think I Saw You...

OFFERING ROMANTIC HOPE TO THE SHY AND CRIMINALLY PERVERTED

I stood behind you on a busy Jubilee line train to Stratford on a Tuesday morning. You smelt so entrancing. I licked your lapel without you noticing. Drink?

To the brunette working in PC World, Uxbridge. I bought a wireless internet card from you, but whenever I try to connect it just says "This programme is not responding". I still have the receipt, but I forgot to ask for your number. Fancy meeting up?

To the kooky redhead I met in the Buddha Bar. You bought me a drink, and showed me your killer dance moves. We shared a taxi home. I made fun of your labia and you got the night bus back. I'd love to see you again.

You: John Snow. Me: the man who sent you some pubic hair in an envelope. Want to come round and see my paintings?

OOGLE BOBBLE AND THE FICKLE BRITISH PUBLIC
Ricky Gervais

'Flanimal' favourite Oogle Bobble gets into all sorts of scrapes when offered the chance to work on some big budget productions in America Land, but is dismayed when his old friends stab him in the back and decide he isn't funny anymore.

Comes free with the DVD of Gervais's new sketch show "Awkward Situations Involving Gays, Racial Minorities and Disabled People".

THE LITTLE GIRL WHO DIDN'T HAVE TITS
Katie Price

Heart warming "ugly duckling" tale about a 7-year-old girl called Clara who travels the world searching for the perfect bust, with a bit of magical help from enormously bosomed fanny-merchant Jordan and her surgeon, Dr Fariq!

Comes with a free can of mace.

BOB THE LABOURING PROLETARIAT
Julie Burchill

Abrasive simpleton Burchill is never afraid to tell it like it is, and this re-imagined instalment of the popular "Bob the Builder" series doesn't disappoint.

The irrepressible Bob swears his way through another mini-adventure, spurred on by a head full of unworkable Marxist ideals and his mantra "Can we fix it? Only if the Bourgeoisie ceases to exist!"

FUNNY 'N' FEELY BOOKS: THE RISE AND FALL OF THE THIRD REICH
Simon Schama

A great hands-on book for kids who want to get to grips with the horrors of Nazism. Give them a feel of Hitler's bristly moustache and they won't stop giggling!

THE POP-UP BOOK OF TURGID MORTALITY
Will Self

Thoroughly oppressive, but beautifully colourful, Self's new book is sure to inspire the imaginations and deep-set anxieties of the nation's toddlers.

I SPY...FISCAL STABILITY
Gordon Brown

A great picture book for pre-schoolers consisting of page after page of Microsoft Excel spreadsheets from HM Revenue and Customs. It's up to your little ones to spy the erroneous data!

TOMMY THE NONCECATCHER TRILOGY
Danny Dyer

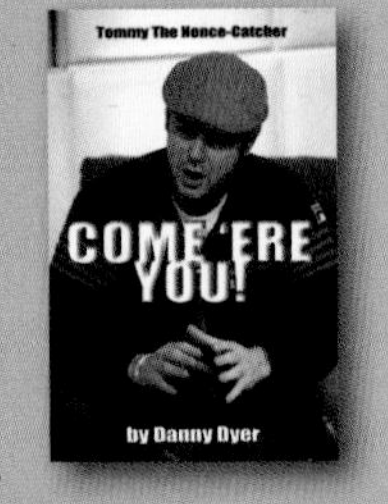

Look beyond the remedial spelling as the raw danger of 'nawty London' is seared onto your child's retina by loveable scamp Dyer. This edition contains all 3 works - "Com'ere you!", "What you playin at you nonce?" and "'Ave some of that".

GLOSSOP THE HAPPY PIG AND HIS ATROPHIED, HUMBLING DEATH
Hugh Fearnley-Whittingstall

Wonderfully veiled paean to a rural idyll, which ends with a promise of "no Christmas presents" to any child who doesn't write a letter of complaint to Tesco. A great book - think Babe meets the Mark Thomas Comedy Product.

(DON'T) COLOUR-IN GUIDE TO THE KORAN
Martin Amis

Gleefully naughty iconoclasm from Britain's favourite novelist and kiddy writer. Make sure you DON'T open the attached free crayons.

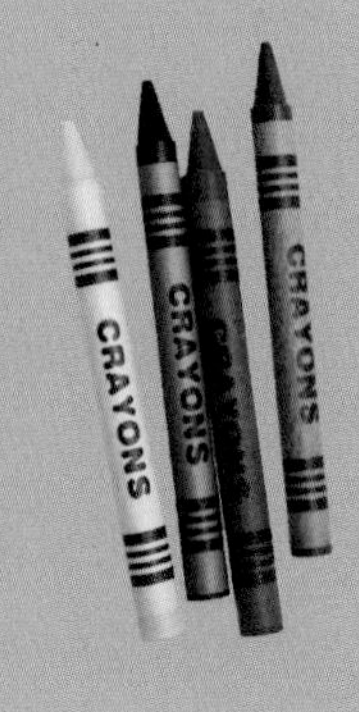

Lonely? Sad? Worthless?

Read yourself better with London Shite's self-help book chart...

Be Your Own Muesli

Control + F, Replace:
How Excel Can Improve Your Emotional Decision-Making

'I Just Can't Go On':
A Personal Tale Of A Life Much Worse Than Yours

To Me, To You:
Cheery Office Teamwork - the Chuckle Brothers Way

Sun Tzu's 'The Art Of War' For Assertive Librarians

Machiavelli's 'The Prince' For Long Distance Hauliers

Would You Like Another Cup Of Tea?:
How To Cope With Someone Coping With Bereavment

CELEBRITY BIOGRAPHY BARGAIN BASEMENT

How We Watch

We know our readers don't like to spend hours surfing the TV wave for choice channels. That's why we've designed our own London Shite Digi Top-Up card, giving you access to our 4 favourite cable channels, which all embody our WAFT philosophy...

Weighty – BBC Four -1

High-culture made complex, BBC Four -1 delivers all the same artsy content but with the audio track played one hour behind the visuals. Deliberately obfuscating, usually baffling but enthralling for some, this fascinating concept forces you to think, in a medium that rarely does so. Can you still concentrate on that documentary about Palladio with the distraction of a Tom Waits concert providing the sound? Find out today!

Ambitious – Sky Sports Comment

24-hour football-based cultural banter, this high-brow addition to BSkyB's sports coverage sees writers, poets and film-makers questioned whimsically about the burning sports issues of the day by polo-necked newsreaders. Watch out for the flagship show 'Butcher, Baker and Seminal-Film Maker' where wizened ex-pro Terry Butcher, portly funnyman Danny Baker and a different film director each week discuss the silver screen and the Premiership in equal measure. Watch online for a classic episode where David Fincher totally lambasts the concept of the transfer window.

Fun – Lummy!

Because we all like being fun sometimes, Lummy offers the now-est music video smashes in handy 20-second bites for when you just can't be bothered to think about anything other than bejewelled hoes and their gyrating flesh. If you're bored at any time press the red button to see lovable tomboy Pink singing nursery rhymes.

Thought-Inducing – 'The Man Who...' Channel

For viewers who want to spend more time sympathising with other people's freakishness than Channel 4 allows, this brand new emotional sponge of a channel offers non-stop documentaries about the most compelling of bodily misfortunes. Make sure you stay in for the Friday night line-up, which includes 'The Man Who Ate a Bicycle', 'The Man Who Had One Leg Fatter Than The Other' and 'The Boy With Moira Stewart's Face'.

Budget TV

What the hell do they spend the money on?

	BBC ONE: £1.4bn	ITV1: £900m	SKY ONE: £150m
Biggest one-off purchase	£85m to create the 'Davies Project': a new BBC department which produces, films and edits every single thought imagined inside the brain of TV genius, Russell T Davies.	£75m to boost ratings for 'The Bill' by casting Vin Diesel and Susan Sarandon as two young cops learning the ropes at Sun Hill.	£7m on scalp ointment for Ross Kemp
Naughty Expenditure	£4m to jet-pack Mark Thompson back from Tuscany every Sunday evening.	£7m on Michael Grade's humidor.	£5m on 'gangs' for Ross Kemp to be 'on'.
Plans For The Future	£40 million to make the iPlayer accessible in space.	£4m on re-developing 90s smash 'London's Burning' set during the Great Fire of London in 1666. Robson Greene to play Samuel Pepys.	£2m on 'The Crips on Ross Kemp': a 24-part series where the notorious LA murder-based gang follow Kemp around as he goes to auditions and does some shopping.
Gift to Legends	£10 million for Andrew Sachs' *Apologia* Stairlift.	£3m on taxidermising David Jason for the ITV lobby.	£3m on prosthetic limbs for Kiefer Sutherland to ensure 24 can live beyond its 12th season.
Nod to the High Brow with...	£2 million on 'golden shackle' for David Tennant, tethering him permanently to a vending machine in White City to stop any contact with ITV.	£2m for a special 'Southbank Show on Ice' extravaganza.	£1.5m on 'Really LOST': a discussion show hosted by Gavin Esler accompanying the 9th series of the US smash where newspaper columnists attempt to explain the plot and in some way relate it to US foreign policy.
Ferret about in the Lo-Brow with...	£4m on 'Harmless Banter Tap' to replace Adrian Chiles on 'The One Show'.	£1m to research 'Bash Her! Britain's Funniest Domestic Abuse Clipz'.	£1m on 'Sexy LOST': a plot-free edit of each episode featuring none of the tricky dialogue but simply a 26-minute montage of the most attractive members of the cast running about all hot.
Gazump SkySports with	£6m for live and exclusive coverage of Lewis Hamilton playing XBox with his school friends.	£2m to pay for housewives' favourite Steve Ryder to interpret live Premiership football matches through expressive dance.	£4m on live coverage of 'World's Most Risky Yachts'.
Celebrity Poach	£0.35 for Colin Murray to add celtic tomfoolery to 'Question Time'.	£2m for George Alagiah and Kelly Brook to present 'Lush News at Ten' in tight jeans and vests.	£0.25 on Dale Winton's chiropodist to keep Noel Edmonds sweet.
US Import	£2m on 'Limey Spooks': a US remake of the BBC smash featuring the exploits of Sir Rupert Boffington and his band of Round Table Spies.	£3m on exclusive rights to every film featuring a performance by Billy Crystal.	£1m on 'Faulty Wire: Da Krazy Shit!': a hilarious portfolio of outtakes from unanimously popular Baltimore drugs cop drama 'The Wire'.

Have A Scoff, In TV's Trough

BBC Four launches 80s season with a special one-off documentary...

DANCE ON ICE

Classically-trained, sour-faced actor Charles Dance analyses his hero and close friend Vanilla Ice with the help of celebrity interviews and stunningly accurate historical reconstructions.

ALEX ZANE'S BOOK WANK

After brilliantly harnessing the capricious and inaccessible nature of the "World Wide Web" in last year's "Rude Tube" on Channel 4, the Zanester follows his success up with a look at ready-books.

In this 6-part series, Zane uses the medium of television to guide the viewer through exactly how, why, and where books exist and what they have done for the world.

Episode 1: Over 48 hours, Chaucer's "The Canterbury Tales" will scroll across the screen word-by-word, while illuminating witticisms and helpful tips from a freshly-trained Zane guide us around potential pitfalls.

Left: Zane (who often accidentally glues his hand to the back of his head) argues that books are "pretty ace".

The coming year promises to be a fine vintage for all things small of screen, so we've put together a *London Shite* guide to our favourite shows...

THE UNCOMPROMISING SCOTTISH POLICEMAN

Gritty, hard hitting crime drama in which a shouty detective behaves like a bastard to everybody but eventually arrests someone who's been abusing kids, so isn't really a bastard after all, but sort of is.

Guest stars John Virgo as Jimmy the Rapist.

READY STEADY COOK: REDUX

The ever cheerful Ainsley Harriot brings a bit of extra spice to the competitive cookery show by forcing contestants to whip up a three-course meal in some of the world's most hazardous environments, including a collapsed oil rig, a sinking ferry and a contested Afghan opium field. While the chefs fight for the condiments, and for their lives, Ainsley circles the arena in a helicopter shouting instructions and impressions of his Jamaican mother through a megaphone.

LILY ALLEN'S NOOKS AND CRANNIES

The nation's favourite BMX-riding popster tours various UK buildings and is challenged by members of the public to fit herself into spaces that normally couldn't accommodate a fully grown human being. Episode 1 sees Lily getting into difficulties in a primary school air-vent in Surrey.

THE NATIONAL LOTTERY – LIVE FROM BELMARSH PRISON

Eamonn Holmes makes the public's dreams come true in front of the country's most dangerous criminals.

EASTENDERS

All hell breaks when new character Martin Luther arrives in Albert Square spouting inflammatory remarks about the rights of the baptised and universal priesthood. Meanwhile, Bradley is furious when he is sold an overripe pear.

FLASHBACK! WITH BRUCE FORSYTH

New Saturday entertainment in which members of the audience try to convince a confused and heavily sedated Bruce Forsyth that they are members of his family come to visit and make him remember events that never really happened.

LAST OF THE SUMMER WINE SEASON 58

In the war-torn future of the Yorkshire Dales, a bionically enhanced Compo still relentlessy stalks his killers from season 7, and the villagers struggle to put on the summer fete when a mysterious virus starts eating away at their faces.

PAUL AND DEBBIE'S SUNDAY NIGHT TAKEAWAY

Wizened ex-king of light entertainment Daniels and his slowly bloating wife Debbie are filmed by CCTV cameras in their Cheshire mansion each week as they attempt to order, collect, pay for and consume a meal from a local Chinese eatery.

This week: Paul forgets to ask for Hoisin sauce and has to sleep with the dogs.

FIDDY IN THE MIDDLE

Watch an ultra-competitive Curtis '50 ("Fiddy") Cent' Jackson playing popular child's game Piggy In The Middle with a different class of inner-city primary school students.

This week: Mrs Oliver's Year 4 of Our Lady of St Cross, Balham. Justin Lee Collins presents.

JAMIE OLIVER'S CHEEKY FOOD APARTHEID

Fed up with people demonstrating less culinary scruples than his good self, Jamie commandeers a grotty Northern town and turns all the cook-not layabouts into a subservient underclass.

Episode One: Jamie limits suffrage to those who can produce a technically perfect crème anglaise.

WHAT NOT TO CHAIR

Newly besuited, Trinny and Susannah class up their act with this handy new guide to running a successful meeting. In this episode, sparks fly when Trinny and Susannah clash over the merits of whiteboards vs OHPs.

VIETNAM VET

Chris Barrie crosses the Atlantic and puts on an American accent to play a war-scarred veterinary doctor whose curmudgeonly character conceals a genius for curing sick pets.

HOW TO LOOK GOOD HUMILIATED ON NATIONAL TELEVISION

Far too many women have silly hang-ups about how they might look having their hideous muffin-tops pinched and prodded on national TV, so inhibition-smasher Gok Wan steps in to tear their pitiful rags off anyway and force them on an empowering nudey bounce down Oxford Street riding a golden Space Hopper.

DON'T MISS!

MISS BUT RECORD!

BBC FOUR WITH THE ENO PRESENT

l'Academie des Policiers

The complete Police Academy epic cycle as originally devised by Verdi

Carey Mahoney - Steve Guttenberg

Eugene Tackleberry - Bryn Terfel

Moses Hightower - Lemar

Total Immersion Season

now in eye-prodding

TETRIS

THE MOVIE

Any Noise Will Do...

BBC One announced plans for the upcoming new year's schedule, with music-based tear-yielding reality shows predominating more than ever before.

HOW TELLY BROKE THE MOULD

KEY MOMENTS OF SOCIAL LIBERATION

Taboo broken:

SEX

Taboo Buster:

Grandstand Special: The Royal Copulation (BBC1, 2005)

Ever faithful to the monarchy, the BBC took extra steps to endear the Princes Charles and Camilla to the British public by broadcasting extended coverage of their wedding-night intercourse to millions of licence-fee payers. From 11 o'clock onwards BBC 1 offered non-stop live coverage of the newly-weds' bed chamber, with commentary from John Motson and post-coital discussion with Alan Hansen, Alan Shearer and Mark Lawrenson. As Motty's immortal words "Well, he won't be pleased with that performance" echoed around the nation's living rooms, we all knew television would never be the same again.

Taboo broken:

9/11

Taboo buster:

Taliban(ter)
e4 (2001)

Written and filmed in mid-Autumn 2001 with smoke still rising from the ashes of Ground Zero, this terrorism/comedy hybrid wasn't just a PR disaster for the new youth channel but also an entertainment flop with co-hosts Noam Chomsky and a burqa'd Russell Brand falling out during rehearsals. It did at least remind us how to laugh and mock during those awful times.
Dropped by network after the 'Paul Ross incident' when the producers sent the erstwhile entertainer on a 'banter' trip to Kabul to read a porn mag in a Taliban-controlled mosque.

Taboo Broken:

FATS

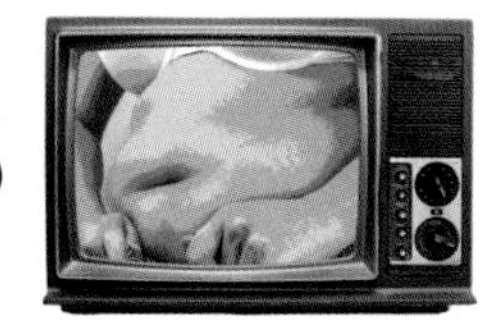

Taboo Buster:

Waddle Bus
(ITV, 1989)

Years before pity-sponging shows like "Celebrity Fit Club" and "Half Ton Mum" hit our screens, short-lived light entertainment show "Waddle Bus" had already exposed Britain's growing obesity problem. By turns funny and upsetting, the show's simple premise saw Jim Bowen disguised as a London bus driver pretending to pick up fat people at bus stops, only to speed away whenever they tried to board the vehicle. Needless to say the ITV secret cameras were always there to capture the saggiest of passengers as they desperately attempted to catch up. The show was cancelled after 3 consecutive strokes in a single episode.

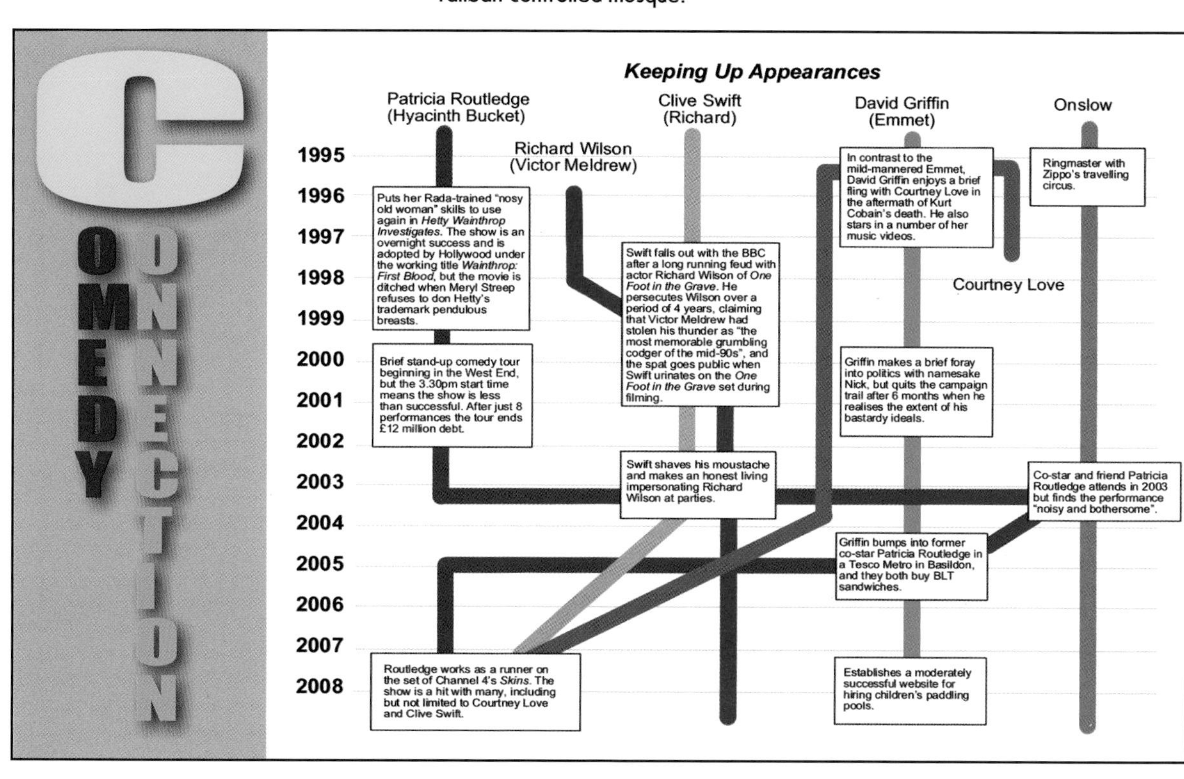

chumportal
all the nice times for interacting

For those of you who find MySpace too urban, and Facebook too full of simpletons, ChumPortal is a brand new sharing space for your loftiest thoughts and intentions. Members of the exclusive next gen social networking site can only join by written invitation, while the baffling design, illogical navigation and seemingly useless applications give it a delicious mystery reminiscent of a Masonic ritual.

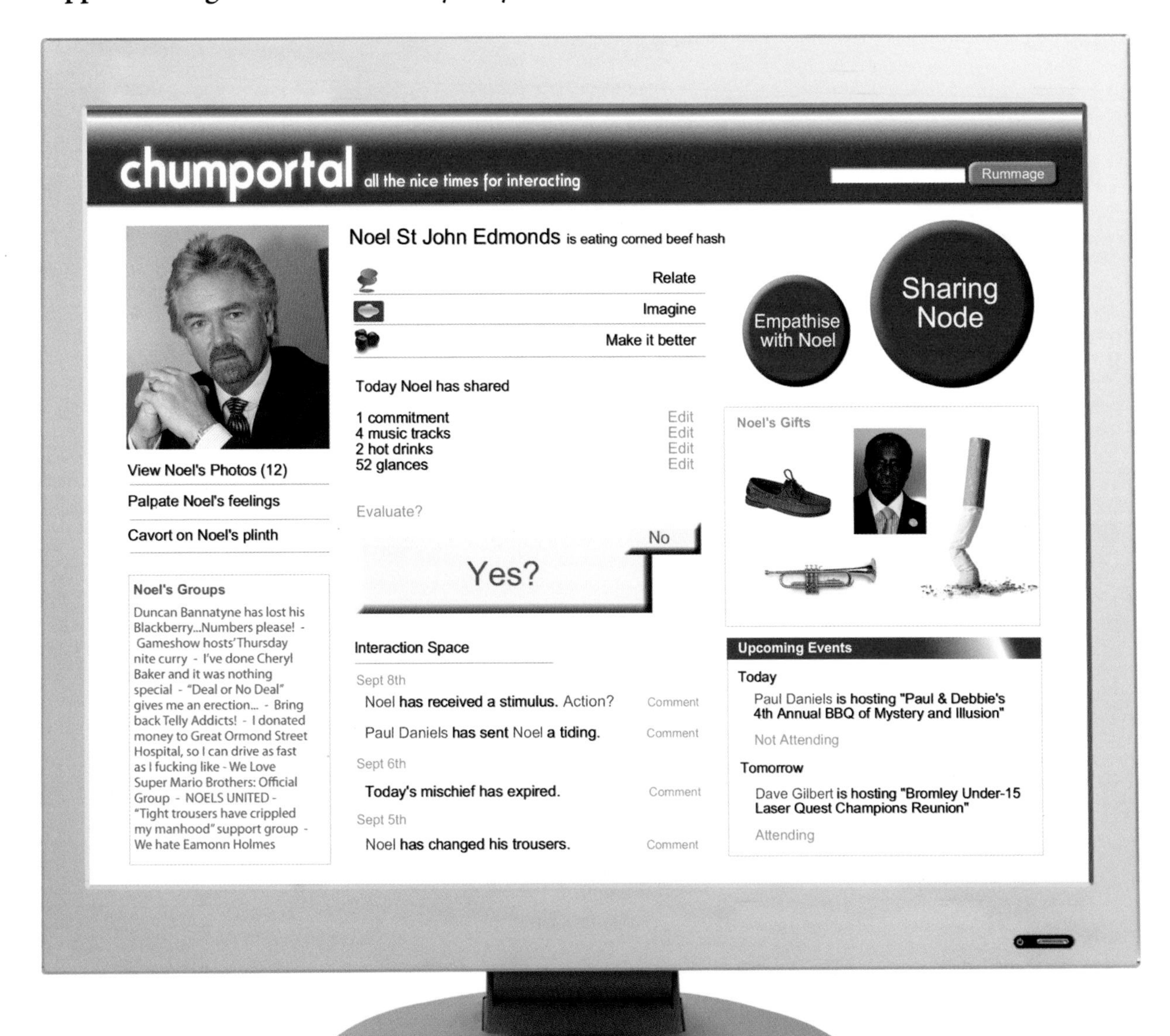

CERE-BRILL!

Train your brain to wisdom and happiness

It's amazing to think for the first 6 millennia of civilisation humanity neglected to tap into Brain Training, now regarded as one of the most obvious sources of better. Here you can find out just how each part can be improved and the products and exercises needed to take you higher.

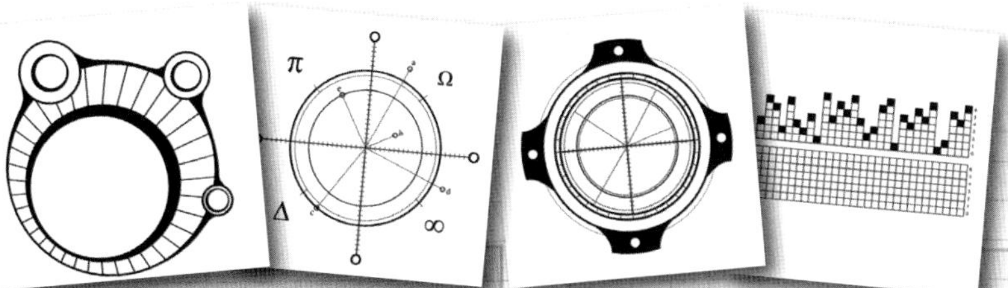

BRAIN DISTRICT: NEBULOSIA

WHAT DOES IT DO?: THE NEBULOSIA IS THE UNSURE, VACILLATING PART OF YOUR BRAIN. NEXT TIME YOU'RE DEBATING WHETHER TO HAVE A SECOND GLASS OF WINE OR SEND THE KIDS TO PRIVATE SCHOOL IT WILL BE THE NEBULOSIA THAT'S HOLDING YOU BACK.

HOW CAN I TRAIN IT BETTER? GOOD NEBULOSIAE NEED CLEAR, STRONG THOUGHTS. WITH THE 'OPINIONS' EXPANSION PACK CONTAINING THE FORTHRIGHT VIEWS OF 8 SINGLE-MINDED AND HEADSTRONG FIGURES INCLUDING NICK GRIFFIN, DAVID STARKEY AND MARK LAWRENSON YOUR DAYS OF DILLY-DALLYING WILL SOON BE BEHIND YOU.

BRAIN DISTRICT: THE MIND (MENS)

WHAT DOES IT DO? 'THE MIND' IS THE ENGINE ROOM FOR ALL CEREBRAL ACTIVITY TAKING PLACE WITHIN YOUR BRAIN.

HOW CAN I TRAIN IT BETTER? IDEALLY 'YOUR MIND' WILL SURGE LEFT AND VANQUISH THE NEBULOSIA. DO THIS BY GIRATING AND THRUSTING YOUR PELVIS AND HEAD FORWARD AS YOU TACKLE A SUDOKU.

BRAIN DISTRICT: THE BACK OF YOUR MIND (DORSUM MENTIS)

WHAT DOES IT DO? A RECENTLY DISCOVERED CEREBRAL POCKET TO WHICH ALL HARD TO REMEMBER FACTS ARE IMMEDIATELY TRANSMITTED AND USUALLY FORGOTTEN.

HOW CAN I TRAIN IT BETTER? YOU REALLY WANT TO TRAIN THE BACK OF YOUR MIND TO A POSITION OF GREATER PROMINENCE BELOW THE CARP AS SHOWN IN SHADOW HERE. TRY THE ELECTRODE-EMITTING NINTENDO SKULLCAP.

BRAIN DISTRICT: THE CARP

WHAT DOES IT DO? IDEALLY YOUR CARP SHOULD LOOK, AS IT DOES HERE, LIKE AN AMBITIOUS, STRIDENT VERSION OF THE RIVER FISH. A HEALTHY CARP TRANSFERS BLOOD, THOUGHT AND ACTION AROUND THE BODY.

HOW CAN I TRAIN IT BETTER? A SIMPLE GAME OF 'CRANIAL PONG' (AVAILABLE AS STANDARD WITH MOST HAND-HELD BRAIN TRAINERS) SHOULD GIVE YOU THE LEFT-AND-RIGHT MOTION NECESSARY TO EXERCISE THIS PART OF YOUR HEAD.

BRAIN DANGER: BAD BLOOD

WHAT DOES IT DO? THE THING MOST BRAIN TRAINERS FEAR, 'BAD BLOOD' IS THE SANGUINARY CONSEQUENCE OF TWO OR MORE PARTS OF YOUR BRAIN NOT GETTING ON AT ALL.

HOW CAN I AVOID IT? TO AVOID THIS CONSEQUENCE OF OVER-TRAINING MAKE SURE YOU GIVE YOUR BRAIN A PROLONGED PERIOD OF BANAL NON-EXERCISE EACH DAY. STARE INTO THE MIDDLE DISTANCE AND CLAP SLOWLY FOR TWO HOURS.

Console Yourself

Computer games have almost seemlessly replaced log-fires as the muster point for the nuclear British family. Most of this can be attributed to humanity's preference for pressing buttons to keepig warm, but some credit has to go to the gamut of games on offer. Here are our picks...

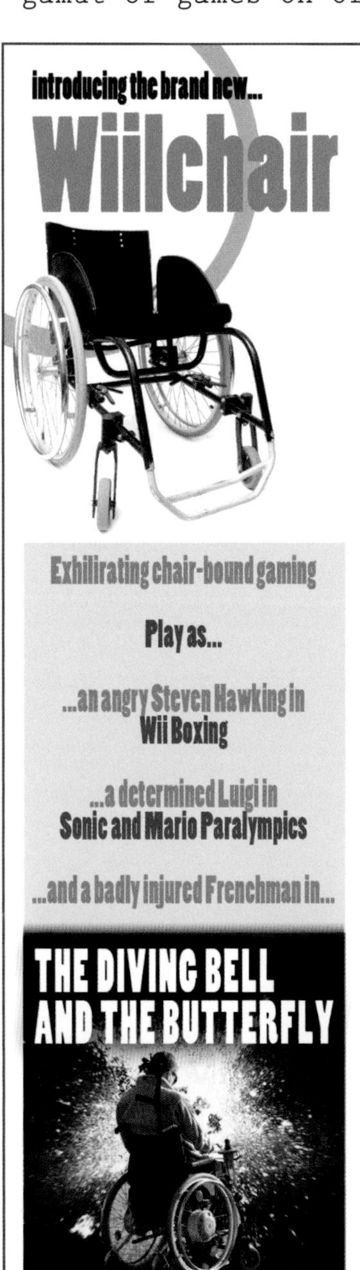

VIRTUA DENTIST
PlayStation3

From the team who brought you Virtua Fighter and Virtua Tennis comes a game that drops you straight into the sterile 3D world of oral hygiene. Battle against your mates head-to-head or online in a host of challenges from the Brace Fitting Time Trial to the frantic Wisdom Tooth Wipeout, performing as much expensive, unnecessary surgery as you can along the way! With three carefully graded mouths to choose from - Overindulged Child, Nightclub Bouncer or Gypsy - it's great for all ages and abilities.

WORLD OF WOOLCRAFT
PC/Online

Enter a mythical realm of heroes, witches and monsters - all of whom need warm, functional clothing. Take on the role of Thorak, a lowly serf, and learn all the necessary skills of knitting, weaving and other loom-work to keep your townsfolk fully clothed. Despite the contrived fantasy setting, which plays no part in the actual gameplay, World of Woolcraft gives you real life practical skills and a seemingly unending range of weaving styles from the Portuguese Underlay to Victorian Crab Stitching.

FOOTBALL MANAGER: ARABIC FUNDS EXPANSION PACK PC

The first of 2 expansion packs for the perennially popular Football Manager series fills your manager's coffers with disgustingly large sums of money, allowing you to buy unlimited numbers of world-class players and cruise effortlessly to the final stages of every major competition. Although serious gamers will quickly tire of the lack of challenges, the initial rush of mindless cash-frittering is a real blast.

FOOTBALL MANAGER: GIFT SHOP EXPANSION PACK
PC

For those gamers and footie fans who feel that the Football Manager series doesn't quite stretch their administrative skills, this expansion pack gives players the more robust challenge of managing the staff of the gift shop, trophy room and canteen as well as the players on the pitch. Organise staff rotas, price items correctly, even have a go with the hoover when employees are thin on the ground, and keep your stadium spick and span while you battle for the championship.

"YUM YUM"
Wii (Japanese Import)

Baffling but strangely compelling livestock-feeding game that has taken Japan by storm. You take on the role of Yuko Ori, a magical creature somewhere between a cat and a trumpet, who has been assigned the task of administering brightly coloured energy pellets to various farm animals. Feed the animals properly and Yuko Ori will sing and dance before your eyes; give them too many wrong pellets, though, and face the wrath of time-travelling robot Megazoid.

COR ANGLAIS HERO: WORLD TOUR
Xbox 360

Ever dreamed of rocking the Royal Albert Hall with your own backing orchestra? Well now you can! Take the stage with the most obscure of all the reed instruments, wowing reserved middle-class audiences with your virtuoso solos and smart attire. Using the Xbox's unique Cor Anglais replica couldn't be easier, with the instrument's 18 valves replaced with 40 different coloured buttons. The games includes a repertoire of over 160 classic pieces, including Claude Debussy's Nocturnes and Bellini's Il Pirata. So get on the tour bus, meet the fans, and rock out - Cor Anglais style!

MAVIS BEACON'S 'LOOK BUT DON'T TOUCH' TYPING
PC

The world's most notorious typist returns with her latest package, specifically targeting the pubescent male. As her young students progress in speed and accuracy, Mavis gently removes an item of clothing accompanied by increasingly loud and suggestive moans of encouragement. 80wpm gets you a happy finish.

Top 3 Cheats

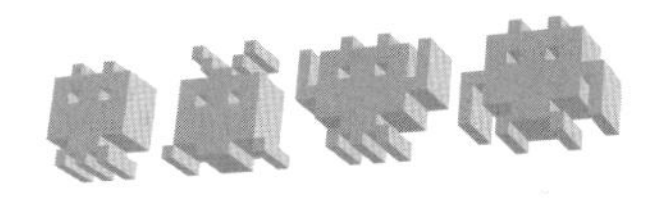

Tekken 6

BONUS CHARACTER

While your opponent is in mid-air, toggle your reverse flipper until you hear a gentle hiss (all the while ensuring your power flap is unselected in the main menu). With your left hand, stimulate X vigorously until your eyes cross involuntarily, and you lose all control of your bladder. Then with Y active or primed, use your tapping shaft to spell out your name in basic morse code. Hey presto! You can now fight on as an irate John Prescott.

Grand Theft Auto

RADIO 4 TUNER

To be able to tune in to your favourite R4 shows from ANY vehicle in the game, simply obey all traffic regulations for a whole year, get yourself a comfortable job, buy a loose-knit cardie and spend weekends setting up some kind of outreach programme to tackle the appalling problems facing much of the inner-city youth.

Wii Fit

SKIP A LEVEL

To skip a level on Nintendo's Wii fit, try actually leaving your house and dusting off your withered 'limbs' on some kind of walk.

E4 Gives Blyton A Massive Skins Graft

E4's sex-and-acne-based teen romp 'SKINS' has re-defined the way TV looks at teenagers. Here we preview 2010's most highly anticipated teen remakes showing just how much SKINnier they've become...

This is the Famous Fuckin 5ive - a rabble of renegade GCSE students who move to Kirrin Island, the only place in the UK where their electronic tags cannot be activated. They bond with a local boy after seeing him mocking a lame dog and form a dystopian unit based around cheap drugs, rough sex and sweets.

Writer Bish Foster takes us through how the show came together...

CHARACTERS

"We wanted to put Enid Blyton's middle-englanders into post 7/7 British life with all the modern shit, but also keep the linear purity of each of those characters. Here's how we storyboarded the 5ive cast and re-worked them into their 2010 incarnations..."

THEN		NOW
Dick – cheeky, loves ginger beer	SKINS>	Rik – cheeky, loves crack
George – tomboy, fiery temper but very loyal	SKINS>	Alex – conflicted bisexual, rabid sex fiend, smoker
Julian – leader, intelligent, forthright	SKINS>	Monkey – leader, can do human beatbox
Anne – youngest, gets flustered, does the group's menial tasks	SKINS>	Akhil – most ethnic, ironically abused, good cook
Jo the Gypsy girl – wild and carefree, especially friendly to Dick	SKINS>	Jo the Gypsy girl – wild and carefree, likes to suck off Rik

PILOT

"When we focus-grouped some of the themes we were discussing with a cross-demographic of teenagers the two words that came up most were "really" and "sex". We tried to create a screenplay that put teenagers in a place they understood but just a lot more shiny. The story begins when Rik does a really cool skateboarding and everyone thinks he's pretty amazing. We quickly flash back to when he shat his pants at the prep school fete and then we're back into the action. Rik uses his slick moves to score a date with Alex but she's got to be with Caleb who's discharged himself from hospital even though he's totally depressed. Rik briefly packs in the skateboarding and thinks about joining the RAF (the plane is symbolic here) only to bump into Akhil at the corner shop. They talk briefly about how amazing drugs are before discussing the innate flaws in the UCAS process. A combination of the balmy summer's night and the cheap vodka leads to a passionate argument and they end up having sex. Akhil is pretty sure he's done an HIV in Rik so he goes to try and get some advice from Monkey. Monkey is hustling a posh boy by pretending he's rubbish at Crash Bandicoot and everyone thinks he's really great again. They have a morbid discussion about sexually transmitted diseases then Monkey gets a text from Alex which she accidentally sent and was really meant for Jo. They end up having sex"

DIALOGUE

Bish explains...

"...dialogue is a teenager's currency. It's pretty much the only route out of their status quo that they have - it's almost also like a car in that sense. Even teenagers with a car will still find dialogue very important, so we spent years listening and documenting the cadence of teenage 'flow' to make sure what we said was what could have been said."

Here's an extract from the scene where Monkey has to buy some great drugs or it will just be a really tiresome night...
Drug dealer:
"What do you want kid?" (immediately he scratches one of his balls in a threatening way)
Monkey:
"I want to get off my face - properly, a big one. No messin'. I'm talking the absolute. You get this?"

SEASON FINALE

Bish continues..

"if you don't have a season finale where almost every perception of each of the characters changes then you're not doing your job. Here's how we've set up our ending - it has to be brave, ambitious and original. The 5ive have returned from the V Festival and found the portal which might get them off the Island but it's being guarded by the police (who represent adults and authority). While Monkey is struggling to work out how to use Blackberry Messenger the key to his moped gets stolen by the police and now the group have no access to fun or swift movement...

....Another Skinful?

With runaway success predicted for the Famous Fuckin' 5ive, the youth production company Dongbusters have already been commissioned to re-immediatise another classic for the more tawdry teens of 2010. We asked director Judd Beaks to fill us in on his remake of Edith Nesbit's timeless children's novel 'Five Children and It'.

What's the show?
"So we start shooting in March and it's gonna be called Five 'Children' and I.T. - basically the 'Children' is in quote marks because they're totally not children - they're teenagers but they've got so much experience beyond their years. One of them was abused by their dad and another one has been to New York."

What's the concept?
"Basically it's about 5 really poor teenagers who find this computer that teaches them how to win at online poker. Soon they've got all the cash they want but their lives have changed forever."

What's the plot?
"Ned and Sascha find the magic computer after they've just had really massive sex next to a factory. They tell Smudge, Pippin and Claude only cos they're their best friends and also cos Sascha secretly quite fancies Claude. There's a brief subplot where Smudge can't find her phone which is all tied into the fact that she hates her mum. Anyway, Pippin and Smudge have a big fight and they end up having sex. They start spending the money the magic computer has made for them and there's a really great scene where they do sick on a career advisor's tie cos they totally don't need him. Then Pippin dies from a fit and everyone wonders if it was all worth it but after the funeral they all sing a song and it's fine."

London Shite Piracy Crusade

Sure, back in the early noughties taking a cheap, easy toke on the piracy pipe was pretty fun; we all downloaded a few albums or bought a knock-off DVD from a shifty Chinese down the pub. But now this must stop and we must grow up.

Here we highlight a few of the main campaigns being used to raise awareness for this sick art-destroying obsession...

Twatter

Is your life too immediate to labour over the 100 characters Twitter offers?

With Twatter, your blogging can be 10 times more micro! Keep your friends and fans updated with the minutiae of your gimcrack existence in nice'n'easy 10 character communication nuggets.

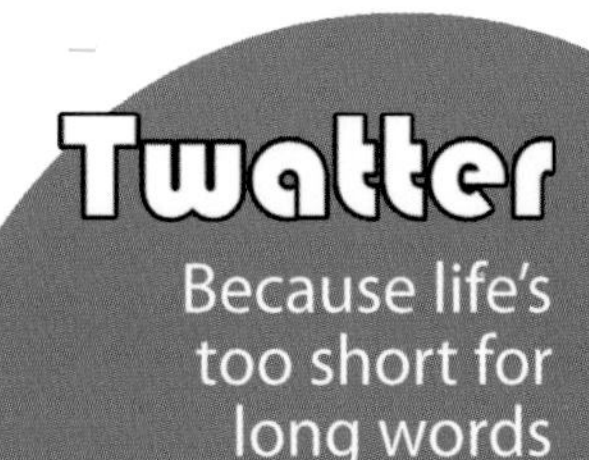

CAMPAIGN: WATERWORLD TORTURE

TARGET: DVD COPIERS

CONCEPT: With the current 3-minute long anti-piracy film that prefaces all DVDs having a negligible effect, the BBFC will replace it with Kevin Costner's maritime epic *Waterworld* in its entirety. Anyone watching a retail or rental DVD will now sit through all 136 mins of this 1995 classic with the words: "PIRACY. REALLY BAD" emblazoned on the screen throughout.

CAMPAIGN: THE CEEDEES

TARGET: ILLEGAL MUSIC SHARING

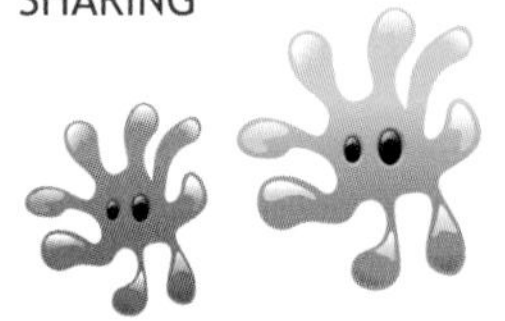

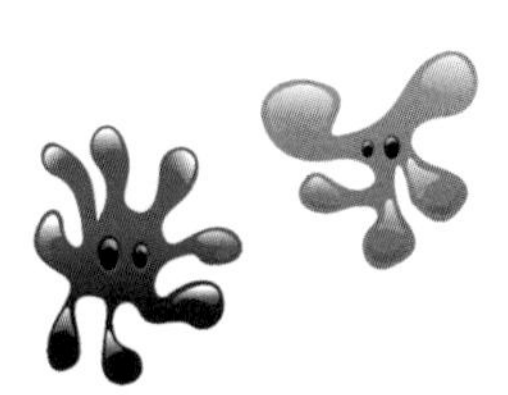

CONCEPT: To make people more guilty about whoring their CD's precious songs around the internet, a virtually-rendered family of magic jelly beans have been designed to symbolize this soon-to-be obsolete audio form.

TAGLINE: You wouldn't burn your pet, So don't burn me!

CAMPAIGN: MYRA THE DOWNLOADA

TARGET: DOWNLOADING FILMS THROUGH THE INTERNET

THE CONCEPT: When 2008's 'Knock off Nigel' only served to fuel burgeoning interest in the growing sector of web-based torrent downloading, firmer action was needed. The result was a viral campaign aimed at teenagers surfing torrent sites, which saw a 4-D projection of the noted child-abductress Myra Hindley appear on the screen and slow mouth the word 'Naughty'.

TAGLINE: What? You didn't mean it? That's what she said.

CAMPAIGN: WHAT THE PDF?

TARGET: CHEAPSKATES WATCHING FREE PORN

The campaign: 'You know the type of guy who never buys a round or chips in for a present or pays for a porno film?' - so begins the blurb for the latest campaign by the world's pornographers to stop stingy and aroused young men from getting off on free adult sites. 'What the PDF?' will convert all downloadable AVI clips into painstakingly slow PDF documents rendering the users enjoyment utterly flaccid.

TAGLINE: Don't scroll like a wanker. Buy some porn.

This Is Viral

It seems these days like you can't go a single day at work without someone forwarding you a brilliant video of a child falling off a bike or a man blowing his own face off with a firework. This is "viral". Thanks to the internet, today any Tom, Dick or Mimsy can take some grainy footage of his uncle fondling himself and post it on YouTube for all the world to see and applaud. And before you know it, the clip is a smash hit and Uncle John's groin is the new face of Pepsi Max.

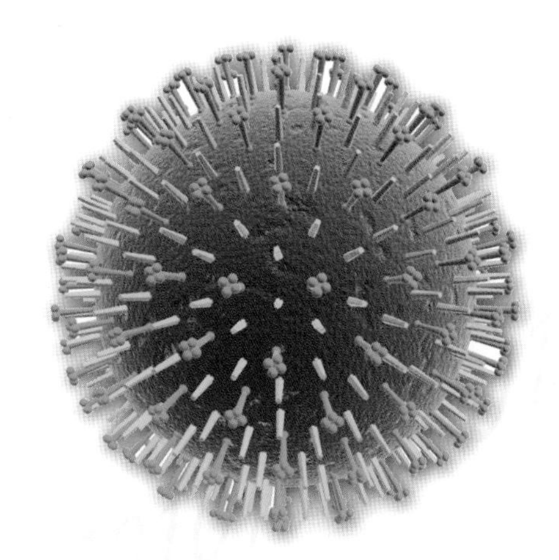

Here we take a look back at the revolution of viral :)

SUCCESSFUL VIDEOS

Who can forget these classics? Lol!!

STAR WARS KID – Loveable film seen by millions of an enthusiastic young Star Wars fan cavorting with a lightsaber made from a broom, then having a minor stroke and needing to be resuscitated by paramedics.

DOG IN A BRANDY GLASS – Inspired by the adorable "Kitten in a Brandy Glass" video, this cute little film documents a toddler's efforts to stuff a fully grown labrador into the same vessel (with mixed success).

TOPSHOP ADVERT – Of course viral is a great advertising tool for getting to those hard to reach demographics. Cheeky Topshop reproduced the harrowing Vietnam epic Apocalypse Now but with all the characters wearing their new range of skinny jeans – and the video spread like Agent Orange in the South East Asian jungle!

WHOTUBE?

Once upon a time we all headed for YouTube to get our dose of multimedia funny. But a whole host of Tubes that cater for the most exacting of tastes have sprung up in its wake. Here are just a few:

SUETUBE – The internet's most extensive archive of Sue Barker footage, including a previously unseen black and white film of her meeting Hitler.

PHEW!TUBE – Hilarious collection of videos of fat people getting uncomfortably hot in various scenarios. Check out "Dawn French Trapped In Sauna", it will have you giggling all day!

STEWTUBE – Nothing but videos of stews and casseroles being prepared, cooked and eaten. There's some good trivia in there too, like HotLentil458's "Top 10 Frasier Episodes Involving Stew".

FLUTUBE – Thought provoking video site broadcasting footage of bed ridden individuals blowing their noses and moaning about how they can't hear anything. Watch the old man sneezing set to Radiohead's "Street Spirit (Fade Out)" and prepare to be moved.

TUBE STATS

Young adults in the UK spend more time watching viral videos than they spend swallowing.

1 in 3 primary school children have seen internet footage of an animal mounting a household object.

Scientists calculate that the total amount of thought that has gone into creating all YouTube videos is roughly comparable to the amount of thought the average person expends when opening a carton of milk.

88% of the world's population have seen "that video of the bodybuilder shitting himself".

EMOTICONFIDENCE

How to make sense of all those cryptic comments:

:) = I'm feeling pleased

: (= I'm feeling displeased

; I = I have a squint, but I am neither pleased nor displeased by it

q: (= My hat is too small, and I am displeased

: {} = I've grown a moustache, and I'm thrilled to bits

: s = I have a mouth ulcer

How We Eat

UNLOCK THE SERCRETS OF UNBRIDLED GLUTTONY WITH OUR DELIGHTFUL SCRUM! GUIDE TO EATING (OR JUST READING ABOUT EATING)

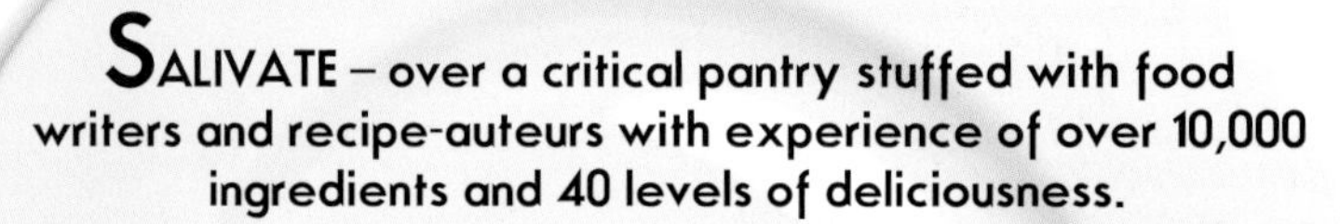

SALIVATE – over a critical pantry stuffed with food writers and recipe-auteurs with experience of over 10,000 ingredients and 40 levels of deliciousness.

CLEANSE – your palate with a refreshing boule of urban sorbet, perfectly offset by a citric shard of pithy glibness.

REALLY ENJOY– a hearty steak of incisive comment, balanced precariously on a bed of celebrity cabbage and all just dripping with 'couldn't give a fuck' sauce.

U TELL US – what you think through our public opinion pud – a stewed mass of dough that's covered in sweet self-righteous custard but leaving a distinctly bitter aftertaste.

MAKE IT ALL DISAPPEAR! – with a refreshing tisane of dietary recommendations, and helpful tips for coming to terms with your bloated, shameful body.

CelebrEATy Sauces

In the beginning there was just Paul Newman and Lloyd Grossman decorating our pasta, but now we've gone absolutely crackers for sauces made by knowns. Here are our faves for 2010...

Kirsty Walk's Grillin' Sauce

Give your lamb-chops the same saucy piquancy followed by harsh-grilling that Kirsty's *Newsnight* guests endure on a nightly basis. Perfect for post-Book Club supper.

Barry George's HMP Sauce

Invented and refined during George's bleak years as an inmate at Whitemoor Prison, this delicious barbeque number has a doleful aftertaste that makes you think how awful it must have been. HMP sauce has been a cult-smash amongst London's foodies and George's route to a new career co-presenting *Saturday Kitchen*.

Rowan Williams' Pastor Sauce

Deliciously episcopal stir-in sauce dreamt up during breaks at the latest General Synod. Reverend Williams hopes to lure back lapsed churchgoers with the enticing slogan – "put this on your penne and try telling me there's no God!"

Darcus Howe's 'Wo de' black mon' Sauce

Indignant chili sauce from the famously sullen broadcaster and race commentator. Features a 3,000-word essay on the back label entitled 'How Levi Roots has undone the good work of my ancestors with his guitar'.

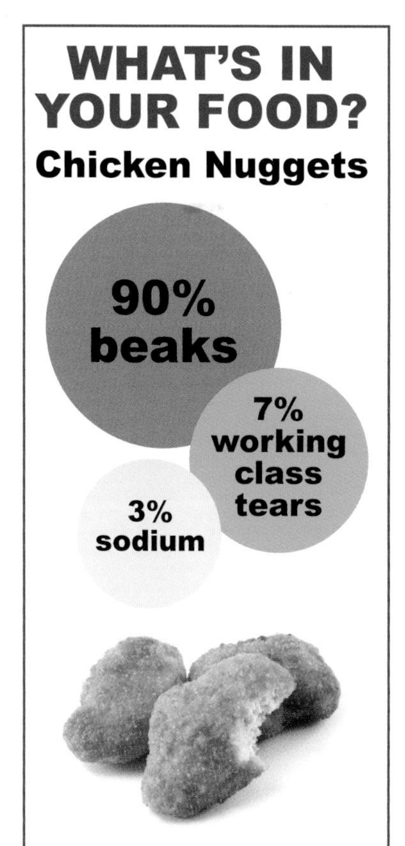

new from Gordon Ramsay...

Chef's Whites Sanitary Pads

"If I was a woman, I'd use these fucking pads to absorb the flow of my menses."

Around the World in 80 ...Utensils

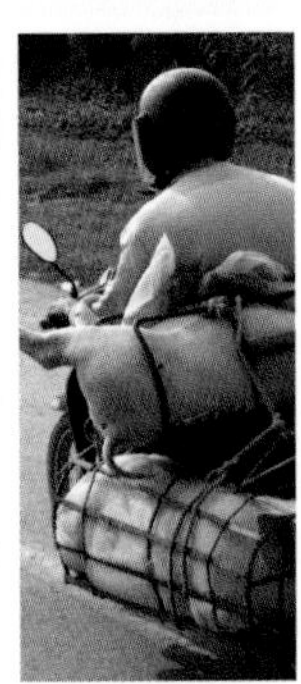

Pretend actor/ explorer, Ewan McGregor, and his friend who nobody cares about are off on another adventure... of the gastronomic variety!

The intrepid duo are taking another BBC-funded gap year, this time sampling the eating habits and extraordinary cutlery of 80 of the world's most foreign cultures.

UKRAINE: Ewan samples the Balkans' traditionally unhygenic cutlery with some poor people, and comes to understand what it's like using the same spoon for soup and pudding in the same sitting.

SAUDI ARABIA: Ewan eats some melon with a really posh fork while his companion watches the bags.

RUSSIA: Ewan visits the hospital and gets flirty with the nurses after his sidekick is stabbed witha fish knife..

COMIC RELIEF SPECIAL: Ewan and his friend who nobody cares about distribute 10,000 forks gifted by Habitat to some of the world's most food-deprived areas..

Follow all of Ewan and the other one's adventures on BBC2 and with the accompanying BBC book.

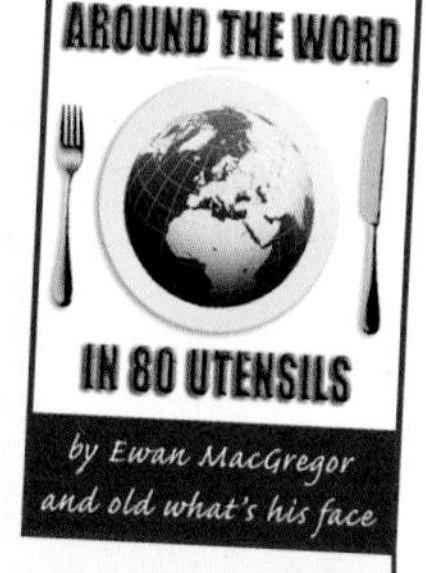

London Shite Lunch Spots

At *London Shite*, 2009 was the year when we got bored of bespoke houmus, pomegranate wraps and all the other tired offerings from London's lunch-eating scene. Here's our guide to the four eateries re-breaking the mould...

Best for fusion: FRAY BENTO-BOX

Do you have the daily lunch struggle between cleansing but paltry sushi and the inertia-inducing stodge of something hot? Fret no more. Fray Bento-Box combines the purity of the Japanese kitchen with your favourite Western gravy-based solids. Each Hokaben Bento comes with a micro-pasty, your choice of inverted pie filling and some tempura corned beef.

Best for poors: OH, CRUMBS

For the small of purse but large of greed, Oh Crumbs! is the ideal lunch-spot. Rather than fill up on a pricey sandwich, diners here can simply chomp their way through kilograms of delicious breadcrumbs discarded by other top-end sandwich outlets. The all-u-can-sup soft drinks trough means they don't touch the sides.

Best for quick and easy: SMUNCH

London's first entirely liquefied lunchery, SMUNCH is harnessing the power of the humble smoothie to render speed and taste happy bedfellows. House specials include Roast Beef and Acai Smoothie with a Horseradish Straw; or the legendary Farmhouse Breakfast Frappucino with Cumberland dunkers. Gullet-widening straws allow lunch to be vanquished in under 10 seconds.

Best for dipping: 1-2-3, EASY AS TSATSIKI...

Soho's answer to the severe cucumber dearth in central London, this yoghurt-based smash claims to have the tastiest version of the dish this side of the Euphrates. Essentially quite cloying in concept and follow-through this is really only for hardcore enthusiasts, although their 'Dipstick' reward programme spurs you on to order more and more.

Give your child the gift of carnal awareness this Christmas. Take them for a yummy day out they'll never forget...

Set in the grounds of River Cottage, Uncle Hugh's Magical Meatopia is set to becaome a mecca for anyone of a flesh-thirsty disposition. Fearnley-Whittingstall and his team of badly painted midget immigrants have gone to enormous trouble to create a land fashioned entirely from the bodily parts and fluids of freshly butchered livestock. Set around a gently flowing river of homemade beef stock, visitors will delight at the fragrant sweetbread rosebushes, juicy kidney trees and esepcially the wonderful lawn of tongues. But there's much, much more...

RIDES!

Enjoy...

...taking the challenge of full-on butchery at Aba-toi?

...finding the courage to clean up the copious animal faeces on Swill He, Swon't He

...experience fun and shame on the Genetically-Enhanced Chicken Buckaroo

EDUCATION!

Learn...

...as Hugh wrestles naked with a blue and white sow (symbolising Tesco)

...about the ephemeral nature of all animal life over a garland Pet Barbeque

...how to tell if an animal is dead or just sleepy

SLAUGHTER!

Recoil...

...while Hugh explains how he likes to film himself slaughtering the geese and watch it back instead of 'boring old cartoons'

...as local retards act out Hugh's harrowing new play, 'Fucked Up Chickens'

Can't Get A Ticket?

Uncle Hugh has hidden 'golden cysts' in five lucky lambs hidden around the country. If you manage to retrieve one, you will be treated to an extra special tour of Meatopia, with one lucky winner spending the whole summer curing hams with the extended Fearnley-Whittingstall family.

New athletic bottled hydration system with Replenish™ mineral ion technology.

- Thames Water PLC certified nutrition
- completely see-through
- isotonic fluid transfer nozzle
- inoffensive watery taste

Every bottle of TAP comes straight from the treatment plant at Beckton, with all the essential chemicals you'd expect from a glass of water in your very own home.

Take it to the gym, give it to the kids – TAP is for everyone.

As drunk by... the cast of Ross Kemp's 'Ultimate Force'.

Going Supple-MENTAL!

Did you know that "food" contains only 30–40% of our recommended daily allowance of nourishment? And while it gives us all the essential vitamins and minerals we need, it gives us only a tiny fraction of the non-essential nutrients that scientists have discovered since the turn of the century.

Luckily a wide range of supplements are on hand to give you the robust, unnaturally protracted life you deserve. Here are our top choices for 2010, as recommended by Doctor Christ Prentice of the Lucozade Institute of Commercial Physicians.

"Smelter's Pantry" Rust Resistant Iron Pellets

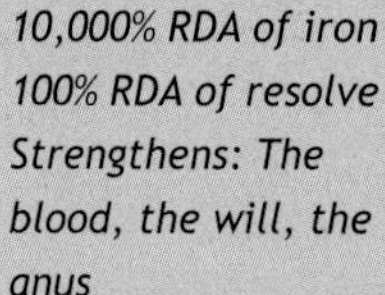

10,000% RDA of iron
100% RDA of resolve
Strengthens: The blood, the will, the anus

Other positives: Pleasant steely taste, sump oil dressing for ease of swallowing

"Treatz" Cod Liver Choco-Shots

100% RDA of naughty indulgence
200% RDA of nougat
10% RDA of Omega 3, Omega 12 and Omega Xtreme

Strengthens: Skin, hair, gagging reflex

Other positives: First supplement that you can make the centrepiece of a girls' night in, while knowing you're staying in great shape thanks to essential oils and uncontrollable vomiting

new from Gordon Ramsay...

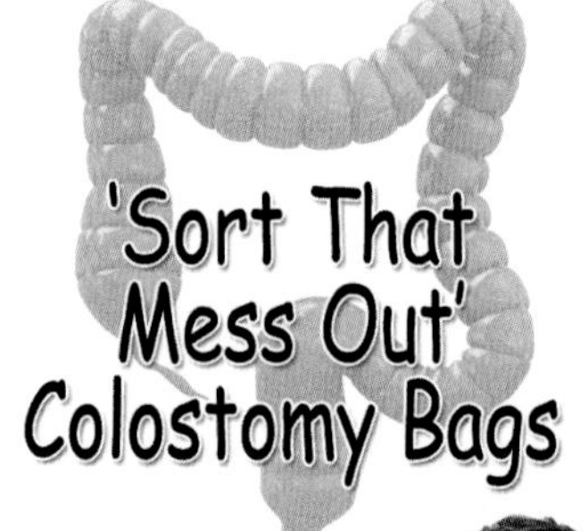

"I don't take any shit - and neither should you."

"Reebok" Maxi-Pump Daily Tabs

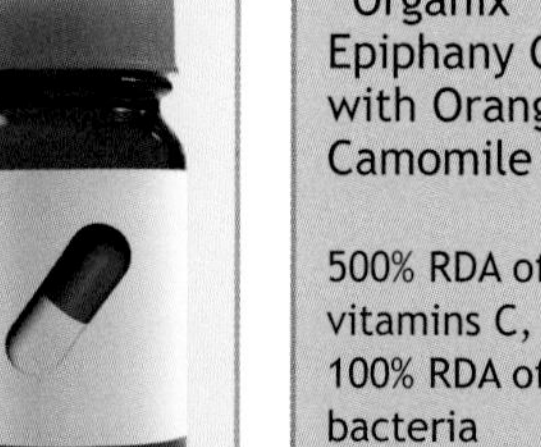

1000% RDA of protein
200% RDA of beta-carbolic mezzanine diphosphate 5 ("steroids")
100% RDA of thuggery

Strengthens: Muscles, bones, spleen, competitive spirit, cerebral sponge

Other positives: Allows the user to work with the enthusiasm of Shadow from 'Gladiators' for 72 hours without sleep, with erection

"Organix" Epiphany Capsules with Orange and Camomile

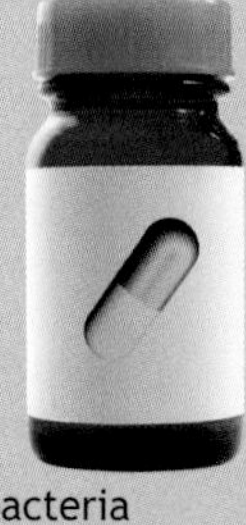

500% RDA of vitamins C, D and E
100% RDA of friendly bacteria
100% RDA of indifferent bacteria
50% RDA of heavenly calm

Strengthens: Bones, hair, soul, belief in gypsy hokum

Other positives: Smells like cabbage, great value, may cause memory loss

Eating out @ Jamie's Living Room

The complete DIY dining experience

Fed up with formal dinners in stuffy restaurants? Get your hands dirty at Jamie's Place, the only venue where you decide every part of your meal from what wine to serve to how to stack the dishwasher afterwards.

All the relaxed atmosphere of dining at home, at high Central London prices.

From the moment you are seated in the restaurant you will be expected to:

- Lay the table under the stern eye of Jamie's mother-in-law.
- Rummage in Jamie's cupboards for ingredients or take a trip to the nearest Sainsbury's Local to stock up.
- Cook three courses in our replica "home kitchen".
- Wash the dishes and clean your table in time for the next customers.

Opening Night Menu

Milk
Samosas
Half an onion
Packet of cloves
3 fun-sized Milky Ways
Something in a tin at the back of the cupboard

Things I Like To Keep Cold

MARIELLA FROSTRUP

TALKS TO DR BASTION SYNGE ABOUT WHAT THE CONTENTS OF A BIG COLD BOX IN THE COOKING AREA OF HER HOUSE REVEAL ABOUT HER EXTRAORDINARY PERSONALITY

MILK – "I love the versatility of milk. Sometimes I put it in my tea, sometimes I just drink it by itself! And it's got that whole minimalist, classic white thing going on."

FAUX-QUORN NUGGETS – "I was so glad when they started producing these. I love the taste and moral superiority of Quorn, but I needed more protein in my diet. These are made from 100% chicken or pork meat which has been treated to give it the taste and texture of Quorn without compromising the nutrition."

MUSTARD – "I eat this with sausages."

HALF A LEMON – "I start each day with a glass of pure, searing lemon juice. It kills all the cells lining my oesophagus and maintains that husky voice that the British public love me for."

SLOW ROASTED SAFFRON OSSO BUCCO WITH HERBS – "Oh God, that's embarrassing! Osso bucco is a real guilty pleasure of mine. I know it has a really bad reputation, but it's great to have something to snack on after work."

TELEVISION REMOTE – "Someone told me that keeping it in the fridge makes the batteries last longer."

DR BASTION SYNGE SAYS:

"Mariella is clearly a complex woman. The milk says 'I'm a calm, rational woman', but the mustard/sausages remark says 'I have no compunctions about hitting people who are smaller than me'. And while the osso bucco dish definitely shows that Mariella is really brainy, her theory about the TV remote sounds like the ravings of a madwoman."

WHAT'S IN YOUR FOOD?

Sausages

70% unsold newspapers (pulped)
28% miscellaneous pig appendages
2% cockney debtors
seasoning

TV SHOW COOKBOOKS

ROSS KEMP ON GANGS (AND WHAT THEY LIKE TO EAT)

With all the grit and no-nonsense determination of his TV series, Ross Kemp offers a unique insight into the diets of the most vicious gangsters in Europe. What's great about this book is the sheer range of recipes on offer, from classic thug favourites like "Scouse Fizzy Pop and Crisps" to a delicious Thai curry submitted by the mother of a people-trafficker.

EAT LIKE A KING – THE TIME TEAM COOKBOOK

A deliciously different take on modern dieting, relying entirely on recipes enjoyed by portly monarchs from the 13th and 14th centuries. Whether you're rustling up a quick plate of Candied Giblets post-gym or having your girlfriends round for Peacock Stuffed with Ox Hearts and a Hugh Grant DVD, this diet really puts the "gorge" into gorgeous!

GRAND DESIGNS GRAND DESSERTS

Accompanying the Channel 4 series, this is a practical step-by-step guide to realising your own dream dessert. The book contains blueprints and detailed wiring diagrams for all of the memorable edifices followed in the Grand Desserts series, including the 40ft marzipan atrium, the shortbread palace at Fishbourne, and the Mason family's notorious meringue windmill that never was.

'OOOOOOOOH! MEAT!' – THE LOOSE WOMEN COOKBOOK

An innuendo-strewn collection of recipes from those sassy queens of daytime TV giggles. The recipes on offer are generally favourites of the 1950s housewife, including shepherd's pie and meatloaf, given a wonderful ironic twist by being made in the shape of genitals. A must-have for anyone who has misunderstood feminist principles or who has understood feminist principles well enough but would rather just talk about cock.

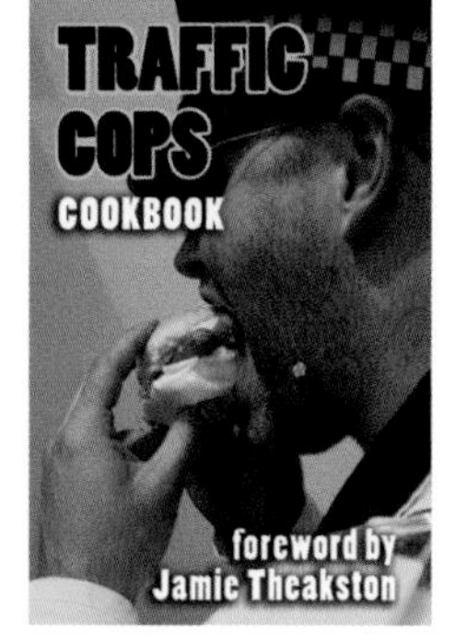

TRAFFIC COPS – HOT SERVICE STATION SNACKS

Ever looked at those mini scotch eggs in their shiny plastic wrapping and thought "Why can't I make those for my girlfriend?" Well now you can! A selection of tasty recipes created for traffic cops who need their grimy food fix when they're off duty. Classics from the UK garage and service-station circuit are painstakingly replicated, including tips on recreating the inimitable offally taste of Rustler's microwavable "beef" burgers and the chemical processes involved in turning regular cheese into cheese-strings. The thought-provoking introduction by Theakston discusses the importance of snacks in modern policing, and how to foil an armed robbery with a Ginsters.

'Luxury Crunch' Sees Massive Rise In Number Of 'Dignity Downgrades'

When the credit crunch hit, all of us at London Shite wondered whether we'd be able to keep on enjoying the 'luxury staples' we've come to love.

Research soon spotted a large rise in the popularity of 'dignity buys' – forms of luxury ingredients high in name recognition and low it taste that allow you to save face and stuff it at the same time!

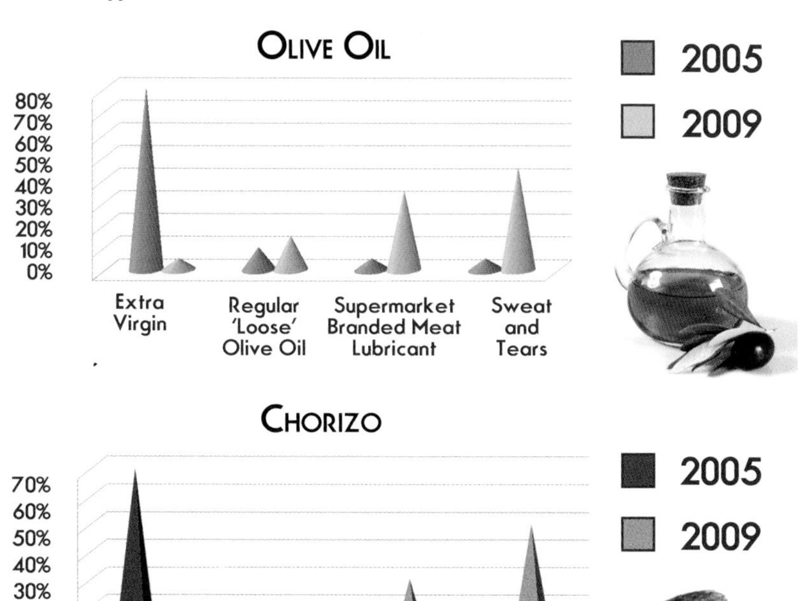

Chorizo

2005
2009

70%
60%
50%
40%
30%
20%
10%
0%

Acorn-fed 'Golden Pig' Chorizo
Swill-fed 'Sad Pig' Chorizo
Sainsbury's Basics 'Cheerio Chorizo'
Rusty Old Spam

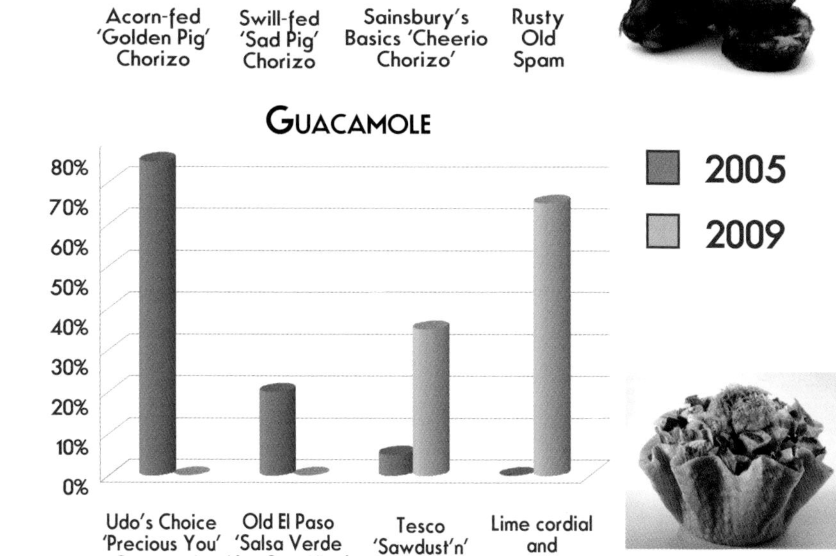

absolve Smoothies

Sin-purging Fruit Loveliness

Tired of having to keep mind and body in shape with the same old fruity mush?

Our new guilt-free super-smoothies are now 100% harmless, containing a unique balance of fruit and vitamins that has been scientifically proven to produce effects "chemically similar to God's forgiveness" and leaving your soul and colon utterly purged.

The absolving qualities of our drinks are down to new growing conditions for our ingredients, in which every individual fruit is given its own sleeping bag and is exposed to nothing but grovelling scripture and the slowest tracks from Kenny G's back catalogue to keep them extra lovely during the growing cycle.

So don't worry your silly head about your sin-ridden mortal frame... we can all be naughty sometimes!

Available in 3 deliciously sanctimonious flavours:

Merciful mango   *Consecrated coconut*   *Pineapple of Holiness*

WHAT'S IN YOUR FOOD?

Energy Drinks

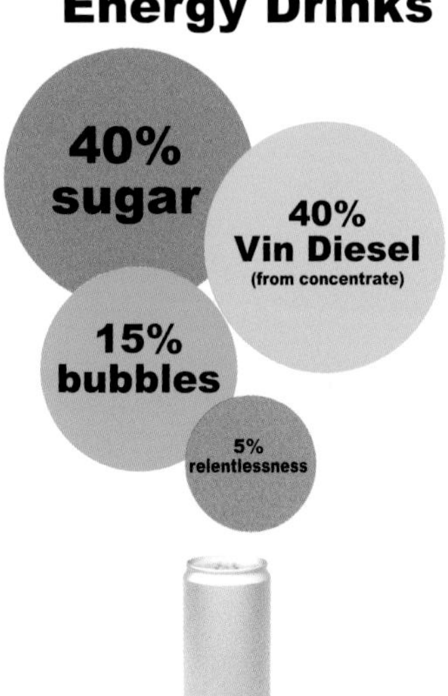

THE SECOND RE-BRANDING OF CHRIST

Catholic Church Launches Holy Snack to Counter Absolve's Menace

At the Vatican, papal legates incensed by the success of Absolve have commissioned 'brand engineers', Think^2, to repositon the tenets of the Catholic faith in the 21st century well-being food matrix.

Too busy for church-based salvation but craving a super-human hit of energy?

'COMMUNION-AND-ON' – a scrummy, Eucharist-based energy nibble delivering an isotonic lift with a little extra push from the great Gym Instructor in the sky.

Contains over 30 times more than your necessary weekly allowance of Communion Wafer and a layer of bitter-sweet raspberry jam symbolising the body and blood of your saviour.

THE HOTTEST NEW COCKTAILS

"The Abi Titmuss"

Literally a must for the vacant hand of any aspirant slapper, this little treat contains vodka, kahlua, egg yolk and three different types of semen.

"The Columbo"

This complex, violet number has so many ingredients that you initially feel quite confused, but once they are fully explained you'll wonder how you never guessed them in the first place. Served in a 6" macintosh overcoat.

"SkidMark"

These babies were being drunk like water at last year's Brit nominees bash. Delicious but potent, this is neat vodka served in a hi-ball with Nutella smeared around the base.

"Favela"

For those shaming moments when you realise just how decadent the act of cocktailing is, this grubby tumbler full of moss, non-branded cola, and mentholated spirits will instantly allay your guilt.

"Bangkok Gang-Rape"

A modern-day, in-your-face reworking of the Singapore Sling featuring Ribena and absinthe.

THE STURDIEST NEW REAL ALES

"Savoury Dreams" (by Bisto)

If you've ever drunk a mug of Bovril and thought "I wish there was a fizzy, summer alternative to this", then your prayers are answered. Bisto have fermented hops, dripping and bits of old cow to create a delicious accompaniment to your pub lunch or just something to dip a crusty loaf in.

"Cardinal's Musk"

A fetid, smoky number served in a genuine 15th-century pontifical hat. The brand has also been officially sanctified by the Vatican as an alternative to Mass wine. The ale has a rich and complex flavour, but contains a level of gas that is almost crippling.

"Soiled Duchess"

This light and fruity ale contains real Devonshire bubbles. Sweet and invigorating to the nose, but producing a bitter aftertaste and a disconcerting itching sensation, the experience is not unlike an unsavoury encounter with a 19th-century London prostitute.

"Old Ian Woosnam"

As lithe and strong as the golfer himself, this ale is brewed by Woosnam on his Staffordshire estate. Woosnam is currently involved in legal proceedings with Scottish drinks manufacture Barr over allegations that he is simply repackaging cans of Irn Bru.

Where did all the cider come from?

2002: Cider rebranded as fun, recreational drink redolent of a mythical sun-kissed Celtic dream-world with which we all feel a connection.

2004: Carlsberg rebrands Special Brew as Special Bramley in an attempt to jump on the apple-y bandwagon.

2006: Kids start abandoning soft drugs, spirits and toys for the apple nectar. The most successful new ciders focus on this growing market, in particular 'Cider with Rosie... and Jim' – a lovable 9% proof "fizzy booze pop" from ITV's favourite ragdolls.

2008: Cider is now so seamlessly interwoven into British consciousness it becomes a valid tool of political discourse. Billy Bragg funds and produces a particularly tart brew branded as 'Whose Cider You On?' with proceeds going to the TUC.

How We Take Flight

SURELY THERE'S MORE TO A HOLIDAY THAN GOING TO THAT TIME-SHARE IN THE ALGARVE AND WATCHING POOR PEOPLE CLEAN THE POOL? YOU BET THERE IS. READ OUR GUIDE TO WHAT'S HOT (BY WHICH WE MEAN COOL, BUT OFTEN ACTUALLY HOT IN TERMS OF CLIMATE) FOR 2010.

ISLE OF MAN – Rich jetsetters are forsaking San Tropez in their droves in favour of this wonderfully ironic destination. Big-thighed popster Rihanna can often be seen here in the summer months stocking up on turtle neck jumpers and enjoying a bout of traditional Manx horse wrestling.

BE A SHERPA – Find skiing a little bit smug and expensive? Many of the poshest destinations in the French Alps now offer Sherpa Deals, which give you an ethnic hat and a free lift pass in return for carrying middle-class families' ski equipment around the resort. Stay silent and they'll throw in a bowl of hot soup, too!

GO CAMPING – The budget family holiday specialists have broadened their horizons with Eurocampz, a new urban camping package. Pitch your tent in the middle of the Champs-Élysées, St Mark's Square or, for the higher budgets, in the bustling foyer of the Vatican to soak up the angry charm of European city life.

PRETEND TO BE JEWISH – Escape the entrapments of modern life with Thomson's all inclusive Kibbutz package. Spend a week fully unwinding with a relentless schedule of worship and ploughing. Although you will only be able to share in the fruits of the Kibbutz if you are Jewish, tour operators have commissioned a Pizza Express and Chicago Rib Shack to be built on site.

From the people who brought you carbon offsetting comes another handy way to assuage your travel guilt

Offset your luxurious holiday stays, fine dining and other shameful travel expenditures by paying for package trips and deep-fried pizzas for Britain's poorest families.

Use our guilt calculator to work out your offsets now!

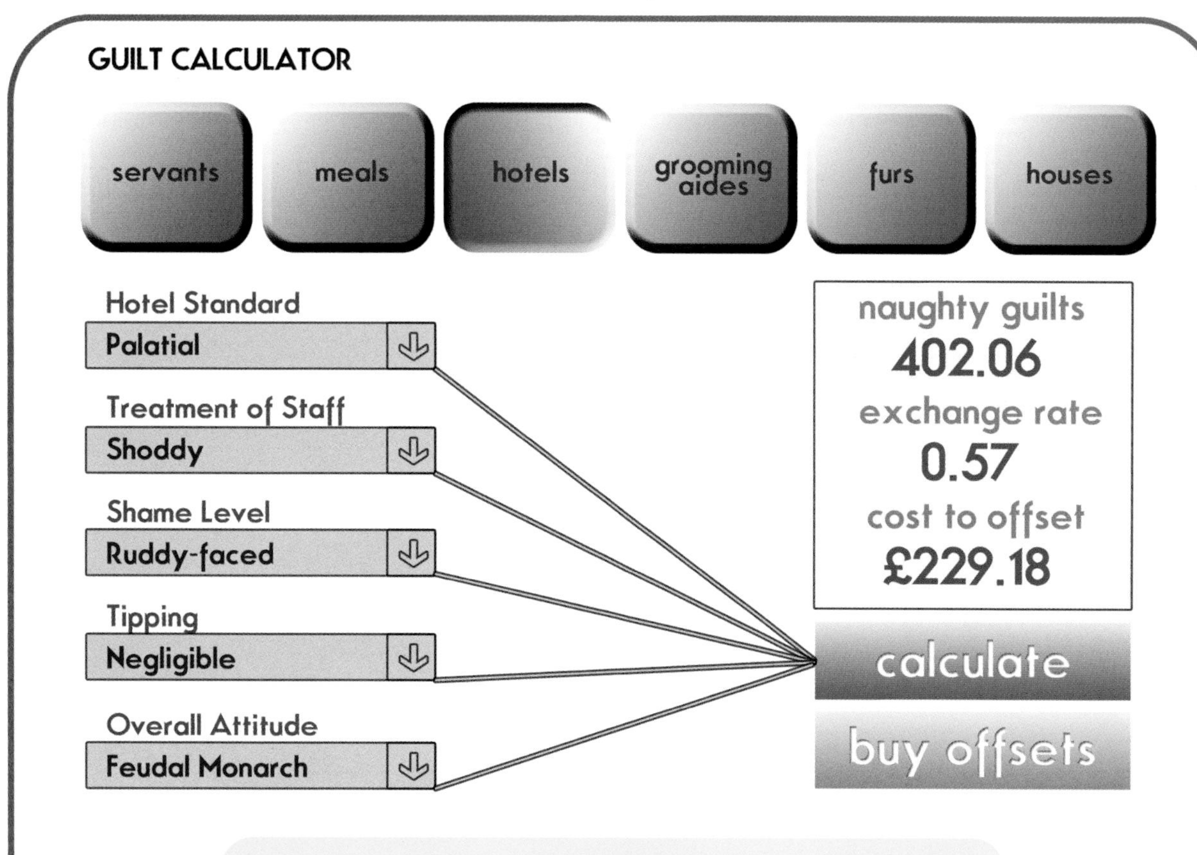

this will buy...

1 trip to Lanzarote for an entire impoverished family from South East London (including Nana)

8 chlamydia tests for an Oldham comprehensive after the Spanish Exchange

20 plates of chips for a soggy single mum worn out by her kids at Butlin's

YES WE AFRI-CAN!

We can all remember where we were that hot day in July 2005 when the worlds of music and celebrity finally rang the death knell for global poverty. But what happened to 'Africa' – the region we were all working so hard to save? The people at Make Poverty History weren't going to allow the locals to get themselves back into a poverty-stricken mess so they sent their best guys out there to sort it all out...

ARABS
(They're OK)

A young citizen of Upper Geldofinland admires an imported piece of Pixie's A-level art coursework.

UPPER GELDOFINLAND

Founded in 2005 and entirely populated by the 100,000 poverty pilgrims Geldof urged to "walk to the equator to demand justice", this area is very much the core of MPH activity. The local poor are encouraged to get over their craving for bread through free bi-weekly art therapy sessions.

LOWER GELDOFINLAND

A more-secluded oasis for The Very Reverend Sir Bob Geldof and his close friends and fellow urgers. Geldof uses the verdant slopes next to the Casamance River to shoot game and drink Pepsi with visiting foreign dignitaries. He bequeathed the small republic of Guinea Bissau to a frustrated Midge Ure in 2006.

The ensemble for Ritchie's smash about a break in at a UN food agency depo, from left to right – Treacle, Noncey, Frank and Diddles.

GUY RITCHIE'S HOLDING PEN

With the poverty removed from so many huge swathes of Africa, whole countries can now be leased out for potential future projects. Guy Ritchie, who hopes to make a naughty gang thriller set in Gabon (telling the story of Africa's potential at the same time), has bagsied this particular stretch of land should he ever find a studio that might fund the project.

'The Starving Girl of Africa' now has rolls of fat secreted in her lower back after years of sugary Western aid.

THE LAND OF THE STARVING GIRL

Birhan Woldu, the hungry child whose notorious lack of food drove Uncle Bob to start this whole thing off, caught the limelight by performing with Madonna at Hyde Park on 'The Great Day'. Since then Birhan has been ensconsed in a gilded ivory cage exhibited to proud Westerners keen to shower her with gifts. Grossly overfed and riddled with rickets, she lives an opulent but sordid existence amongst discarded KFC bones.

ARABS
(They're OK)

SUDAN PLEASURE DOME

Painfully aware of the drought in the Sudan, aid workers quickly set about creating a faux tropical lagoon for its inhabitants. The country is now the world's biggest Center Parcs, covering an area of over 950,000 square miles and offering some of the best mountain biking on the whole continent.

Mabuto the Happy Lion is just one the hundreds of unerringly accurate animatronics on offer to holiday-makers at the Lion King delta.

LION KING DELTA

Concerned that the Democratic Republic of Congo was "misleading" in its lack of faithfullness to "The Lion King", Live8's Rehabilitation Strategists had all the country's wildlife shot or sold to Orlando, Florida, and replaced them with friendly animatronic replicas from the popular kids' film. The entire country was also rigged with tens of thousands of speakers hidden in bushes, piping out stereotypical African "bongo bongo" music 24 hours a day.

CHRIS MARTIN'S MISERY ISLAND

Creatively stymied by the continent's new suffering shortage, Chris Martin set up this misery reserve, where 20 million pre-MPH Africans live out a foetid existence in order to provide him and other Westerners of cultural importance with the inspiration to sound different on the piano.

Jacob loves his branded Coldplay "Yellow" hanky.

AKROYDIA

Funnyman Dan Akroyd accepted the job of hosting 'Live8 Canada' on the condition that he would take charge of and rule the republic formerly known as Lesotho. Fat, balding and malevolent, Akroyd rules his kingdom with tyrannical hubris - espousing a brand of creationism which sees him as the "Maker of Air". He can often be seen stalking his territories with a pistol.

Geografitti: Vandalism From Afar

Bored with the United 'Kingdom' after having already improved most of its surfaces, arch-defiler and prolific think-maker, Banksy, took his little stencil set global. Here are our Top 3 pieces...

No. 1

No. 1 - The Vatican, Rome

Banksy's inimitable 'Pope Benedict XVI Doing Something Implausibly Youth While Being Wildly Blasphemous At The Same Time' is quite startlingly direct in its self-nuanced irony. The work is all the more impressive when you learn that the Pope himself was used as a stencil.

No. 2

I JUST DID A POO POO

BANKSY

No. 2 - The Louvre, Paris

When Banksy revealed he had hung this work in a cupboard at the Louvre for a whole hour without anyone noticing, the art world nearly collapsed. At once gently playful and savagely visceral, 'I Just Did A Poo Poo' was a mortal blow for both stuffiness and artistic skill.

No. 3

No. 3 - The Pyramids, Egypt

No artist in history had ever before used one of the Seven Wonders of the World as a canvas, let alone used one to so effectively deflate Western ideals and values. In 'This Is SHIT and so are YOU', Banksy did more for humanity through 30 secs of work with his trusty paint-filled fire-extinguisher than 100,000 slaves ever could with a few bricks. A truly life-changing oeuvre.

ENGLISH HERITAGE GETAWAYS

While the Crunch may have quashed any hope of holidays to other countries, don't forget you can still get maximum excitement from a day trip to a range of National Trust and English Heritage sites.

NATIONAL TRUST GRAVY MUSEUM – York

Invented in 1655 when Prince Rupert demanded a drink from his cook to refresh him after battle, gravy has a long and colourful history. From the disastrous Gravy Wars with China of the late 1700s right up to the instrumental part it played in the Watergate Scandal, this museum documents the thrills and difficult-to-wash-out spills of gravy's life story. And it's not just about dusty museum displays – the kids can have a great time too, riding on a real-life Victorian gravy train while all you couples can get cosy in the swan-shaped gravy boats.

BRUCE FORSYTH'S PENTHOUSE GROTTO – London

Beautifully restored to the opulence of its 1970s heyday, this is a fascinating, if slightly distasteful, insight into the private life of Mr Bruce Joseph Forsyth-Johnson CBE. The grotto offers a thoroughly British take on the better known Playboy Bunny Mansion, with crystal pickled egg dispensers, a rotating Bovril bar and a solid gold Connect 4 set. Visitors are guided through the exhibition by a holographic Bruce, who explains in some detail the various sexual misadventures that occurred in each area. The gift shop gives you the chance to buy replica outsized playing cards from "Play Your Cards Right" and a selection of Bruce's prosthetic chins.

HOME OF THE MAN WHO MIGHT HAVE MADE THE ROUND TABLE – Gloucester

Delve deep into potential English myth, with this hastily researched exhibition of probable derring-do. Joseph St Simmons was a renowned English carpenter, and may or may not have been aide to King Arthur himself, if he existed. Learn about the exciting part he might have played in the widely discredited legend of the Round Table with the help of historical re-enactments and live carpentry demonstrations. See where Joseph worked, ate and lay with his wife, and imagine how a seminal piece of English myth might have unfolded if it happened. The gift shop is a scaled down Ikea offering round table and chair sets at rock bottom prices.

White knuckle times

The UK's number 1 adventure gift specialist for adrenaline junkies and experience whores.

VALUE BUCKET

Lifted by a big man – £50

Swimming with tied arms – £70

Theory test with Damon Hill – £100

Put in a tumble dryer – £50

Priest for the day – £60

CELEBRITY NAME SHARING ACTIVITIES

The perfect gift for that *Heat*-reading special someone...

– Dog walker with brothers Roy and Murray Walker

– Adopt a seal with Seal

– Go on a ferry with Bryan Ferry

– Cook the perfect meatloaf with Meatloaf

CLEARANCE OFFERS

Swimming lessons with Michael Barrymore

Night shift with the Salvation Army

Xtreme Micro-Scootering

Paperbackpacking

Travel Books For Urbans

"WHOOPS! I THINK I RAPED YOUR PANDA" AND OTHER CULTURAL FAUX PAS by George W. Bush (HSBC Books, 2008) £17.54 + p&p

ADVANCED HAITIAN VOODOO FOR KIDS WITH AIDS by Paul McKenna (False Hope Publications, 2009) £110

31 WORDS FOR SNOW, ONE WORD FOR BLOWJOB: HOW NOT TO LET LANGUAGE RUIN YOUR TRIP TO AN INUIT BROTHEL by Boris Johnson (Bonky Books, 2009) £23.50

COUNTRIES I CAN PROBABLY SPELL - A COMPREHENSIVE LIST by Robbie Williams (EZ Reads, 2008) £1.50 with free crayons

Palin Comparison

only on More4

Part travelogue, part lifestyle advice show, Palin takes you on a mesmerising journey of the world's poorest countries with sytle-guru Gok Wan on hand to point out how their miserable inhabitants are infintely inferior to the chiselled rugby-pitch charm of Michael.

Episode One: Gok administers a Mike-over – dressing an entire Bedouin tribe in khaki flannels and loafers.

BENEVOLENT CRUSADES

JUST ABOUT TO LEAVE UNIVERSITY AND ASHAMED YOU HAVEN'T BEEN TO THE MIDDLE EAST?

EMBARRASSED BY YOUR FRIEND'S BASIC GRASP OF ARABIC?

NEED A LIFE-CHANGING EXPERIENCE REACHABLE ON THE FAMILY AIR MILES?

LIKE MINT TEA?

THEN THE BENEVOLENT CRUSADES ARE FOR YOU.

Our crusades are about unhygienic washing and drinking facility cleansing, not ethnic cleansing (like the ones in the olden days were). We specialise in righteous experience packages for student budgets. Throughout the war-torn Middle East, townsfolk are crying out for clumsy student aid - your mural-painting and essay-writing skills can ease their pain.

PIETY PACKAGE 1: TWO WEEKS IN EGYPT (THE DIRTY PART)

- Travel to a primary school in a shit landrover
- Hand out brightly coloured pieces of card
- Take pictures of laughing children
- 3-day tour of the Pyramids and Valley of the Kings with English-speaking guide
- Includes Economy Plus flights to and from Heathrow

PIETY PACKAGE 2: ONE MONTH IN ISRAEL

- Hang out with students and experience a real-life Israeli Latin lesson
- Learn stories that will give you the moral high ground in any future party scenario
- Watch racial violence unfolding from the safety of the US Embassy's viewing globe, 100ft above street level
- Paint a fence
- Includes Economy Plus flights to and from Heathrow

PIETY PACKAGE 3: SIX MONTHS IN IRAN

- Get to know the world's most notorious almost-terrorist country, sampling their medieval patriarchal attitudes and delicious cuisine
- Arrange a pretend kidnapping to improve your emotional complexity and anecdotal sex powers
- Have a go at making a carpet
- Nod sagely at people you don't understand
- Includes Economy Plus flights to and from Heathrow and a fun teatowel to wear on your head

BOOK TODAY AND FINALLY UNDERSTAND WHAT THEY'RE ALWAYS TALKING ABOUT ON QUESTION TIME!

Do you...

- LOVE fun?
- HATE immigrants, jews, gays and lefties?
- sometimes FEEL so terribly lonely?

You do? Great! Then why not join dozens of like-minded lads looking for love and hate-filled good times on one of our new pleasure tours of some of London's most threateningly diverse areas. Including:

- immigrants in Southall; gays in Soho; jews in Golders Green and lefties in Oxfam.

You provide the mindless hate, we provide the fun ...and who knows what cupid might bring to the party!

How We Sweat

WHY DO WE SPORT? OUR RESEARCH SHOWS MOST READERS PLAY COMPETITVE SPORTS TO WIN RATHER THAN TO GET EXERCISE. HERE OUR SPORTS PSYCHOLOGY GURU DR BASTION SYNGE SHARES OUR UNIQUE **PUSS** FORMULA, IDENTIFYING KEY AREAS TO ACHIEVE MAXIMUM 'WIN'.

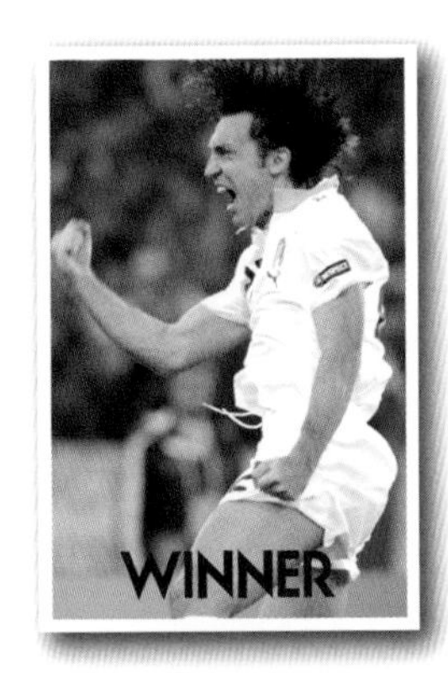
WINNER

PASSION – 'Passion manifests itself in sport through sharp bursts of adrenalin which can yield spiky hair – look at our **WINNER** on the left and his cocksure bonce compared to the sallow look of our embarrassed LOSER. This is why passion-fuelled desire-based athletes like Sir John Terry have vertically impressive hair whilst that of more flaccid athletes like Tim Henman limps along sheepishly.'

UNWILLINGNESS TO FAIL – 'An unwillingness to fail is either engrained in an individual or massaged out of an area below the kidneys. In this case it is quite simply pushing the laces out of our **WINNER**'s shorts as if to say "I will/have vanquish/vanquished this obstacle".'

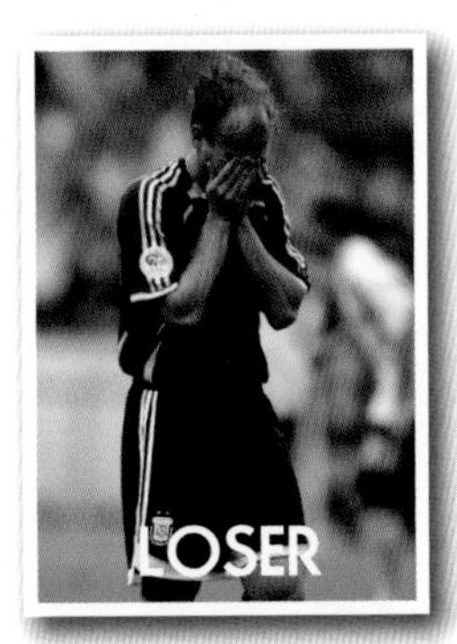
LOSER

STRENGTH – 'Strength is a totally nebulous concept and difficult to measure, but studies show it is in no way helped by covering your face and eyes with the palms of your hands as is happening on the left here. Aim more for the strutting glare of the **WINNER** but beware not to attempt all sports from a side-on stance; it can prove cumbersome.'

SHORTS – 'Shorts now play a major role in 95% of world sports and you have to get that part of your game right or you may as well give up. As you can see from my research, sportsmen who transform their shorts into daring jock-pants revealing thigh and confidence in equal measure will have far greater success than the long floppy nonsense of our LOSER.'

Sport of The Year

AMERICAN football

What You Need

- helmet, carapace, face mask
- energy baton
- nylon running slippers
- cast-iron penalty slippers
- 4x sandbags for defensive line
- 2" pincers (8" at junior level)

Positions on the Field:

Offensive Line
Quarter Back
Double Intruder
Wide Angle Destructor
Narrow Destructor
Wide Receiver
Blessed Receiver
Vortex

The Rules

DESPITE THE FACT THAT MOST EUROPEANS ARE BAFFLED BY AMERICAN FOOTBALL, THE RULES ARE RELATIVELY SIMPLE.

Offense The aim of the game is to get the ball over the opposition line (a touch down, or "downy") in a maximum of 5 phases. One phase consists of 12 action-event points, and each manoeuvre is assigned a certain action-event rating, thus making up a phase. For example, a throw has an action-event rating of 2, but a swipe with an energy baton will have a rating of 6. So a "downy" can be achieved with 10 swipes of an energy baton, 30 throws, or a combination. Running has an action-event rating that is proportional to the speed of the runner. Jogging is illegal.

This all means that all the players in a passage of play have to be observed very carefully, and their action-event ratings calculated. For this reason there are 2 referees for every player on the pitch, which at smaller grounds can make for cramped playing conditions.

Defense Obviously the defending team's goal is to prevent the "downy". This is achieved not only with their bodies, but also through tactical deployment of sandbags. Tackling is performed with the aid of crab-like pincers, usually worn by the Wide Angle and Narrow Destructor – for every second that an offensive player is pinned with the pincers, another action-event point is added to the totaliser.

Teams also have the option of bringing on a special defensive player known as Vortex, who can operate outside of the rules of the game. If a defensive team collects over 100 "blue sky" points, the Vortex can call upon the devastating "Air Strike" manoeuvre.

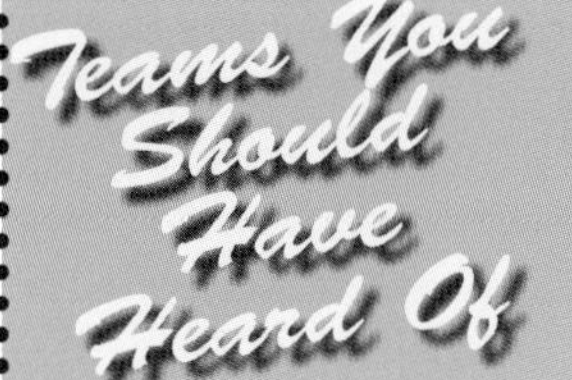

Delaware Mustangs

New York Bellboys

Tampa Bay Tiny-Shorts

Illinois Raging Pelicans

Rupert Murdoch's All-American Pain Squad

Football 2.0

Remember when football grounds were full of piss-stained working classes and cigarette butts? Luckily the streamlined 'sporting pro-audience product' developed by the Premier League means those nasty days are behind us. But they're not stopping there...

Let's take a look at the new teams who'll be playing 'Football 2.0' – the rebranded version of the nation's game – from next season onwards.

THE RISE AND RISE OF THE PREMIER LEAGUE

1992: Idea for new super league hatched in the back of Alan Sugar's executive Volvo estate.

1995: Premier League briefly becomes known as 'The Premiership' for one season before switching to 'Optimum Soccer Occasion' and 'Massive Football Package' for two unsuccessful six-month spells.

1996: Angered by the popularity of the national side at Euro '96, the Premier League briefly threaten war on England before a truce is arranged by Jimmy Hill.

1998: With English hooligans on the rampage at the World Cup, the Premier League tries to calm them down for domestic games by providing free 'Score!' brothels at motorway service stations up and down the country.

2002: The Premier League signals its intent by seeking to become the first non sovereign state to join G8.

2008: "The 39th Step" announced – a plan for total global pre-eminence which would see concurrent Premier League matches being played 24 hours a day in 39 exclusive spots around the world.

TEAM: MANCHESTER BLUE FOR VISIT ARABIAN GULF ALL-STARS

SLOGAN: 'Maximum goal!'

STORY: Backed by the passionate football fans of the United Arab Emirates, this franchise has already assembled a stellar squad including big names from the Premier League, Serie A and the world of light entertainment. A roster of stars including David Beckham, Pele, Andrew Flintoff and an animatronic replica of Bobby Moore will be added to this transfer window with the signings of Vernon Kaye, Wolf from Gladiators and the Spirit of Stanley Matthews. Inspired by watching the DVD of 'Escape to Victory', the ruling Al-Salman family will also attempt an audacious bid to sign potato-faced star, Sylvester Stallone, as the club's flagship goalkeeper.

TEAM: THE INVADERS

SLOGAN: 'You can't take our freedom!'

STORY: In late 2008 Paramount Pictures began purchasing the registrations of all 42 Scottish football league clubs to rebrand them as one single anti-English entity.

Tapping into box-office-proof perceptions of the Scotch race, the team insists on playing with fewer players than their English opposition but through a mixture of skullduggery and aimless long-balls, they are always confident of victory ('freedom').

Team: SALISBURY RED SOX

Slogan: 'It's gotta be Salisbury!'

Story: After actively searching for the right team with which to enter the UK soccer-space, Lake Buxley, owner of the American Football franchise, the Tampa Bay Tiny Shorts, chose to start one from scratch in this charming Wiltshire cathedral city.

Tempted by fantastic marketing cross-over opportunities with the nearby South Wiltshire Museum and Spire FM radio station, Buxley has invested £450m to build a state-of-the-art stadium and conference centre.

Team: MILTON KEYNES ACHIEVERS

Slogan: 'We must prevail'

Story: Owned and managed by Möller Private Equity, a Frankfurt-based finance house, this franchise has set out to become the most ruthlessly efficient team in competitive sport.

With a squad of German and Scandinavian players selected for their 'inability to fail', the team produces saccharine football usually settling games with a single goal celebrated with their trademark 'nod and hand-shake' celebration.

Team: THE BEEFEATERS

Slogan: 'Go, the Beef!'

Story: Devised by advertising agency WPP as a way to boost global awareness of the 2012 Olympics, The Beefeaters have absorbed all the professional football clubs of the Greater London area to create one 'fully-genuine Cockney franchise'.

Sporting a streamlined kit that still manages to incorporate tunic, knee-breeches, tassel and halberd, The Beefeaters will certainly bring some much needed pizzazz to the dowdy world of on-the-field fashion.

Fan of the Match

Celeb fan auction to be centrepiece of new cross-demographic sporting arena.

In 'Football 2.0', it's the star names in the stands that will take centre-stage (the squads of players will be selected at random).
Let's look at some of the star names, who'll be bidding for them and what makes them so special.

ANT AND DEC

Expected value: £45m
Likely Destination: The Geordie Pistols
Marketability:
Look great in scarves
Good at shouting
Demographic reach:
Pervasive

TOM PAULIN

Expected value: £5.5m (part funded by the Arts Council)
Likely Destination: Islington Aesthetes
Marketability:
Half-time poetry readings
Boethian concepts of fortune will assuage sad fans after defeat.
Good banter
Demographic reach:
The Ciabattering Classes

LEO SAYER

Expected value: £15m
Likely Destination: The Norfolk Retrogrades
Marketability:
Still considered trendy in most of East Anglia
Demographic reach:
Restricted to backward peasants

JIM DAVIDSON

Expected value: £1m
Likely Destination: The East London Stereotypes
Marketability:
Has his own tannoy
Demographic reach:
The Threatened

FOOTIE CELEB CORNER

My Top 3 Throw-Ins

by Simon Schama

1. Peter Beardsley to Darren Peacock

NEWCASTLE VS MAN CITY, SEPTEMBER 1994

This scorcher hit Peacock in 30 yards of space. Beardsley, with his insouciant bob and effortless touch, has always reminded me of a young Fra Angelico and this throw-in did little to convince me otherwise.

2. Graeme Le Saux to Nigel Spackman

CHELSEA VS SHEFFIELD UNITED, OCTOBER 1992

This cheeky double-hander enlivened an otherwise dour game – a great throw, with Le Saux's trademark ambivalence between the temporal and safe and the ethereally ambitious.

3. Ruel Fox to Justin Edinburgh

SPURS VS MAN CITY, MAY 1997

It went straight to him. Amazing.

Transfer Records

A RETROSPECTIVE GLANCE AT THE MEGA DEALS THAT BROKE THE MOULD

United Kingdom

1880 - Aston Villa sell left-winger Teddy "Stumps" Hargreaves to the Duke of Westminster in exchange for "a very fine pair of gentleman's gloves".

1901 - Portsmouth FC have a Christmas flutter and buy every inhabitant of Trinidad and Tobago for £40. They then organise a monthly shipment of 5 families to be trained at the club's ground.

1944 - With food scarce thanks to rationing, and any excess frowned upon during wartime, a wealthy Manchester United buy Charlie Suggs from Newcastle for a modest £60, a tin of goose fat and a shepherds pie.

1979 - Trevor Francis is bought by Nottingham Forest for £1,000,000 on account of Brian Clough's misplaced belief that he would give his players unlimited vitality.

1996 - Alan Shearer goes back to Newcastle for a record breaking £15 million in a deal brokered by Pepsi. The corporation agreed to front the money on the condition that Shearer opened and drank a can of Pepsi Max after every touch of the ball.

The World

1915 - Keen to win the Christmas Day Armistice match at all costs, Field Marshal Haig personally sanctions the signing of German artillery officer and centre-forward Jorgen Svard for 10 guineas and the promise of real bread.

1935 - The transfer of Santi Santamaria del Santa Maria from Real Madrid to FC Barcelona for a record 200,000 pesetas leads to shame and disgust on the streets of the Spanish capital culminating in the fainting of a nun. Sold back two years later riddled with syphilis the transfer would be seen by many as the chief cause of the Spanish Civil War.

1974 - The Miracolo della Malanzana - a 7-inch wooden idol of the Virgin Mary believed to be able to attract the attention of Christ - becomes the first 1 billion lira transfer as it moves from a small village in Reggio-Calabria to join Inter Milan's forward line.

1993 - Using up-to-the minute baby-scanning technology on expectant mothers in the favelas of São Paolo, scouts from the Dutch side Ajax complete the first pre-birth signing of over £1m for the soon-to-be-born Brandao Da Silva. Unfortunately for club and family the boy is born a leper.

SPORTS ENTHUSIASTS! PREPARE YOURSELF FOR POTENTIAL GRIEF DEMONSTRATION WITH...

BLACK ARMBANDS

"...BECAUSE YOU NEVER KNOW WHO'S GOING TO DIE NEXT"

Sleek in their design and rich in their emotional symbolism, these tragedy-bands are a must for the modern-day sportsman and sportswoman. Featuring news-sensitive electrodes that alert you just when to spontaneously break into a minute's silence.

For a short period only get one free with every Premier League replica shirt at JJB Sports.

NEW PRODUCT OUT NOW!

GREY ARMBANDS

For those moments of sad-frown rather than out-and-out tragedy these little beauties won't let you down. Next time a former Premiership legend is a bit poorly or Sue Barker has a migraine show you care with a hint of grey.

FOOTIE CELEB CORNER

My Top 3 Kick-Offs

by Kirsty Young

1. John Barnes to Gary Lineker

ENGLAND VS EGYPT, 1990

This was not only technically perfect (Barno flicked it nonchalantly into Gary's path) but also symbolically seminal for modern British society. In the first England international after Nelson Mandela's release from prison, little Johnny Barnes was showing what a new multi-cultural world could do. I loved it.

2. Les Ferdinand to Gary Penrice

QPR VS SWINDON TOWN, 1994

QPR had a swagger back then, when they were the toast of London and every other Saturday Mariella and I would have a big lunch at the River Cafe and then head down to Loftus Road. Les Ferdinand, regal like his eponymous king of Naples, showed me the beauty and wisdom inherent within a great kick-off.

3. Dimitar Berbatov to Robbie Keane

SPURS VS EVERTON, 2007

This was so effortlessly graceful and ethereally thrilling I simply left my seat and walked out.

Top Sporty Tipz

Johnny Wilkinson

TELLS THE KIDS HOW TO MAKE IT AS A RUGBY STAR

Practice only makes perfect when accompanied by grave punishments. When I was at college I would practise passing for 6-8 hours a night, and if I dropped a pass I stabbed myself in the knee with a fork. Sure, it may be causing complications now, but it taught me the discipline required in international rugby.

Sobbing is the best way to warm down after a training session. I don't feel a session has been satisfactory unless it ends up with me crying. When looking for a coach, always find someone who is a great shouter, and remember to tell him all the things you've done that you're ashamed of so he can thoroughly undermine your confidence.

Meat is your best friend. If there is such a thing in international rugby. But it's a great, reliable companion during training. I begin and end every day by eating the hind-legs of an animal with a glass of Yazoo, and I usually put a pork chop or a couple of kidneys in my pockets to suck on during a match.

Bionic enhancements... have really helped me make that leap from a freakishly over-developed athlete to a tireless, inhuman machine. The laser targeting system in my retina can get a bit itchy, but now my heart has been removed I'm a good 2lb lighter, so it's all swings and roundabouts.

Lee Bowyer

...ON BECOMING A TOP FOOTIE HERO

Don't let anyone hold you back, especially brown people. They're a crafty bunch, and will take your parents' jobs if you so much as give them the time of day.

Always practise with people who are weaker than you. At school I used to join in with the small boys. They didn't want me to, and many of them got hurt, but I felt great about myself. I'd also practise my hand-eye co-ordination 2 or 3 three times a day by throwing things at old people.

Eat properly. Don't believe any of this nutritionist bollocks, I got where I am on a nightly diet of Bacardi Breezers and a packet of Frazzles.

Remember football is a mental game. Absolutely mental. You'll almost always end up fighting with someone.

Hit the showers once a week only. If you shower too often it makes you a gay, and that's a fact.

RUNNY MONEY

Just how is lottery funding affecting grass-roots sport in the UK?

In 2008 – Kids; Sports

£2 million spent on primary school boxing equipment, including surgery kits, kid-sized swabs, and tickets to see the WBC World Heavyweight Final for the poorest children.

£250,000 spent on acquiring a stereotypical old Chinese man with a beard for every youth Karate club in the country.

£150,000 spent on wheelchairs for able-bodied children to allow them to attend disabled sports clubs.

£100,000 on throwing objects for comprehensive schools.

£50,000 "Spirit of UK Underachievement" award to Dundee Under-11s Street Luge Club.

2012 Investment

£20 million on solid gold yachts for the victorious Beijing 2008 sailing team.

£1 million on bulldogs dressed as Queen Victoria to line the route of the opening ceremony.

£500,000 on tiffin for visiting athletes.

£6,000 on non-embarrassing suit and shoes for Boris Johnson.

£100 on rollerblades for Lord Coe.

Obscure English Sport Investment

£2 million spent on rebranding crown green bowling as "Lazer Ballz" and new national bowling/ Quasar centre at the Birmingham NEC.

£750,000 to promote Victorian sports, including jellied-eel hurling and running from Buckingham Palace to London's Docklands with a sponge pudding.

£100,000 spent on new tweed for the young people interested in game shooting.

BRAVO presents

when ANIMALS meet BASEBALL

120 minutes of hilarious, unexpected and harrowing clips as those furry critters stick their noses into the USA's noblest sport.

Featuring footage of:

- Hank Aaron mauled by a racoon
- Eddie Murray colliding with a stray horse in the World Series
- Umpires pelted with seagulls

The infamous New York Nicks seal cull of 1989

Plus! Bonus DVD...

when BASEBALL PLAYERS fall over THINGS IN THE STREET

Are you...

SexuallyConfused.com?

Compare all the options and get answers right now with our simple online survey

I LIKE COCKS AND FANNIES

www.SexuallyConfused.com

ASHAMED BY YOUR SEXUAL CONSERVATISM?
KEEN TO PLEASE YOUR BORED WIFE MORE?

FIND THE PERFECT ACCESSORIES AT
WWW.ADAM4EVE.COM

- MOISTEN HER GLANDS WITH A KINKY EXECUTIVE CODPIECE
- GET HER SAYING 'OH, NIGEL!' WITH A PAIR OF SAUCY FISHNET BUSINESS SOCKS
- BAFFLE HER COMPLETELY WITH OUR SATIN NIPPLE TASSLES
- INTELLECTUALISE YOUR SEX-LIFE WITH HIS AND HERS ELIZABETHAN GIRDLES

DON'T DELAY! MAKE YOUR COCK AND BALLS MORE EXCITING OR SHE WILL LEAVE YOU.

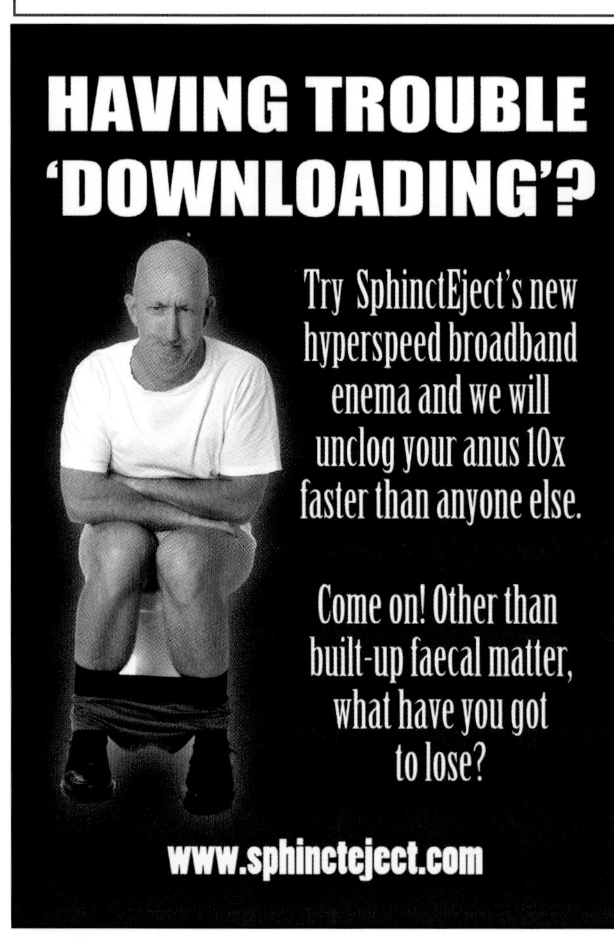

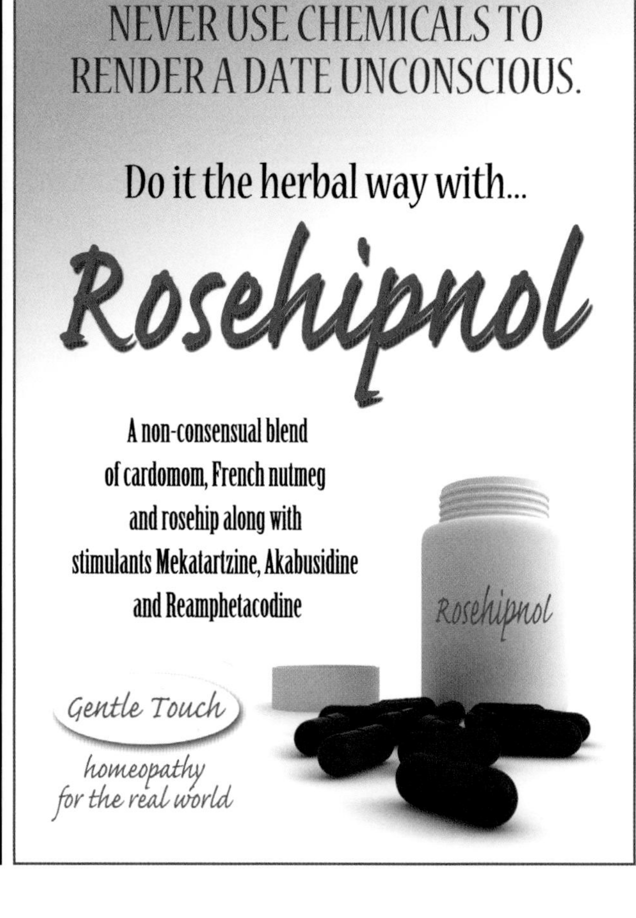

Bored Housewives

Live Chat 5p/min

Banal, parochial chat with hot (and bothered) 50+ women

The emersion heater's broken..0626 461 1111
I can't fit into my jeans any more......................................0626 461 1112
Just got back from Malaga and it was no good...................... 0626 461 1113
Lovely recipe for sponge pudding......................................0626 461 1114
Don't like all the ethnic minorities on the news these days........0626 461 1115

Mistress demands your obedience

Live Chat 1p/min

Whiny, unreasonable requests from sexy girls near you

Clean the bathroom, you pathetic worm.............................0626 300 2251
Make more of an effort to get on with my friends.................. 0626 300 2252
Hurry up and pay the phone bill.......................................0626 300 2253
Stop eating my Shapers yoghurts......................................0626 300 2254

SEXTXT - TEXT SEX FOR LESS,LESS,LESS!

TIRED OF THOSE PRICEY SEX PHONELINES? LOOKING FOR CHEAPER SOURCES OF GRUBBY PLEASURE?

WITH SEXTXT YOU GET THE SAME BUSTY MAIDENS ALL HOT AND NICE BUT WITHOUT THE MASSIVE PHONE BILL AND SWEATY EAR. SIMPLY TXT 844458 WITH YOUR NAME AND YOUR FANTASY AND WE'LL TEXT BACK 160 CHARACTERS OF PURE LUSTY FUN...

FOR THE PRICE OF ONE TEXT WE CAN WEAVE AN EROTIC NARRATIVE TO SUIT YOU...

NAME: DARREN FANTASY: LIKES TITS
SEXTXT: "OOH DRN MY TTS R RELLY BIG N I THNK U LKE IT. U LKE LOOKIN AT MY TTS? ITS A NCE TME 4 U. I HVE REMVED MY BLOUSE N MY TTS R JST LVLY. WE R IN A CAR PARK BY B'N'Q"

NAME: MALCOLM FANTASY: NOTHING FANCY
SEXTXT: "DID U LOCK UP PROPERLY? GO N CHECK MLCLM. GET OFF ME, U STNK OF MINCE. NOT TNGHT. NOT TONGHT. OH OK. QCKLY. HURY UP MLCLM. R U FNSHD? PSS MY BK PLS"

BECAUSE TALK IS CHEAP BUT TEXT IS CHEAPER!

Hello, my friend!

Unsure about the future?
Missing a loved one?
Want to talk to Roy Castle?

I can help. My name is Dr Siri Mahadvayan, and I am a Sri Lankan Tourist Board certified psychic.

I specialise in...

... séances
... tongue reading
... interpreting strangely shaped bread
... wild conjecture

Free samosa with every reading!

LONELY CORNER

MEN SEEKING WOMEN

Attractive, balding, tiny man seeks sympathetic long-armed lady for walks, reaching high things, cinema etc.

Retired Admiral, 67, luxurious moustache, looking for like-minded, outgoing foreigner for a period of superficial friendship, followed by massive sexual deviance. 18-25, or nearest offer.

Mormon hottie, excellent quality sperm, looking for compliant lady with sturdy hips for childbearing and maybe more. Check out my MySpace page: myspace.com/TheMormonator.

Nice time happy man for you (I live Cambodia!! But now Englad is best), you want fuck party? I show you how!!! All sincerely regards.

Experienced gamer, acceptable hygiene, Mortal Kombat champion, needs more than a console for company. Will you press "start" on controller two and enter the competition?

WOMEN SEEKING MEN

Chilled out, kooky girl, 35, excellent track record in providing comprehensive business solutions, seeks similarly free spirited guy who can just make me laugh. Call me between 19:00 and 19:30 on a Sunday. No time wasters, please.

Stunning, feminine Amazonian, used to have balls, looking for understanding man with incurious disposition and a love of films from the olden days.

Princess Jasmine, pure romantic at heart, looking for an Aladdin to sweep her off her feet! That said, I am not hugely keen on men of Arabic descent.

Gorgeous, blonde, 100% non-overbearing divorcee (51, look about 19), seeking replacement husband to organise tours and choreograph dance routines. I am the best thing that will ever happen to you.

Get that classic "I'm wearing a sweater" look with...

THE COTTON MILL

100s of prosaic choices.

Whether worn snugly under a waxed jacket for a stroll with the dogs, or draped provocatively over the shoulders after dinner at a moderately priced restaurant, the mundane, functional charm of a pastel sweater is a perennial favourite with the English gentleman.

Range of colours including

EMERALD LAGUNA
COLONIAL ROSÉ
PROVENCAL DREAMS
PIPPIN
BAXTER
ORANGE WALLOP

Special New Year offer:

80 sweaters for £15 + FREE decorative statuette of Melvyn Bragg

One day he'll grow up to be fat and cocky. Unless you send him to...

BORSTAL

...the UK's most intense training camp for kids of all ages.

If you're worried that he's spending too much time on the Xbox or that she's becoming a bit of a slut and failing her GCSEs, book them in for a fortnight at one of our re-education barns up and down the country.

Perfect for combatting:

- exam stress
- drug abuse
- lopsided gait
- general bad attiitude

If you want to be proud of your kids, try an education with none of the carrot, but a whole lot of stick.

visit www.borstalexperience.com today

Luxury Swiss Terminal Bath

Putting the Ahhh... into RIP

Trouble getting in and out of the tub? Give yourself back the dignity and independence you deserve.

Imagine... sinking slowly into a hot soothing bath, and then very quickly into a delicious coma. Sounds too good to be true? The Terminal Bath offers all of this and more.

Our unique design lowers you in and out of the water with comfort and ease, before delivering a massive dose of tranquilizers to the bather's nervous system. It's just a matter of taps on, and then lights out - making life easier for both you and your family/carer.

100% Swiss made - exempt from EU euthanasia legislation.

Order today and receive a choice of FREE bath salts to drift off to.

If boring old E-numbers can't lift the kids out of a grump, treat them to a little...

PIC'n'FIX

...adding a touch of Class-A to the usual sugar high

Over 20 varieties. Including:

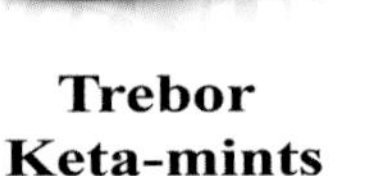

Trebor Keta-mints	Cadbury's Heroins	Vali Yum-Yums	Smarties	Mmmmmm! DMA

All 100% bona fide good shit!

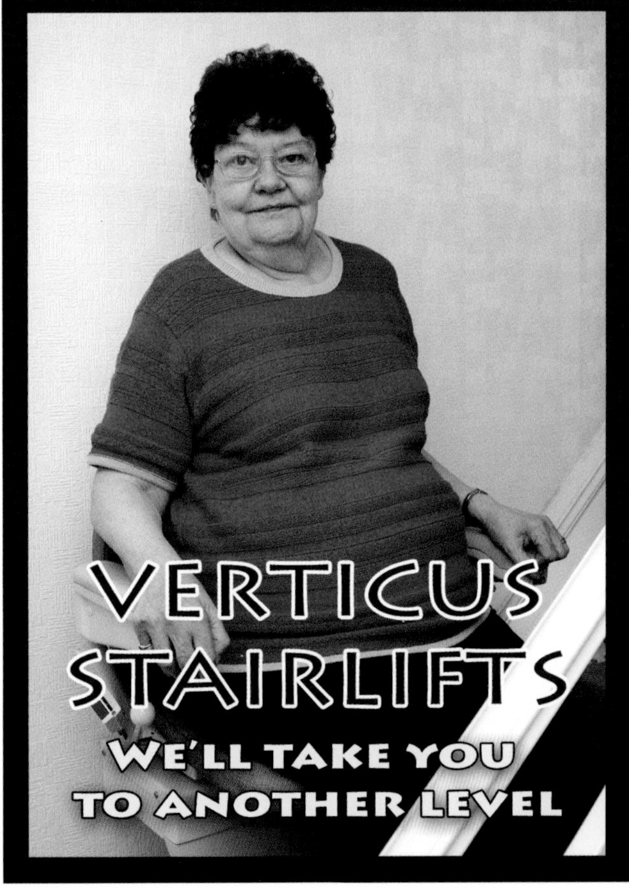

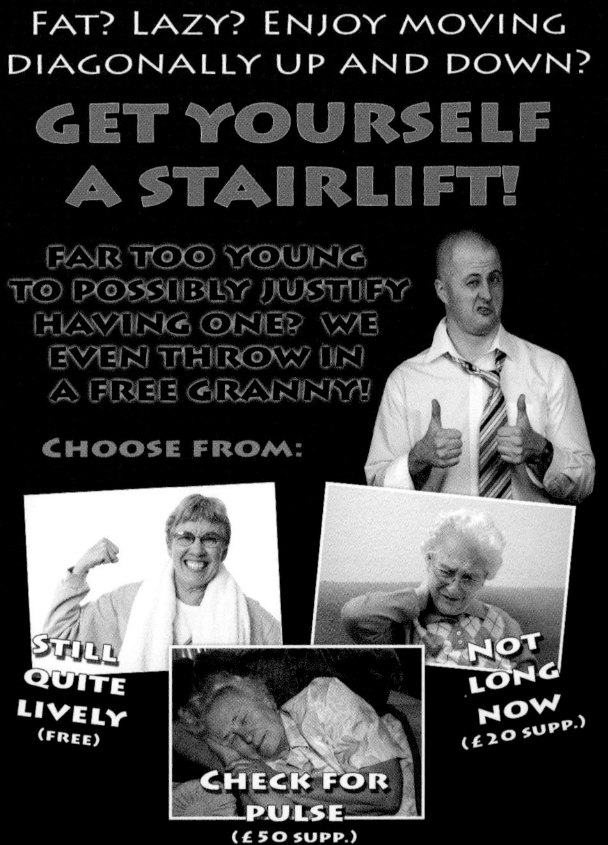

FINAL SCORE

The Complete DVD Box Set

2,234 weeks of football scores across 400 DVDs, all in an attractive Des Lynam shaped presentation pack.

Relive classic, clearly enunciated scorelines including:

"Eastbourne Borough 0 - 0 Ebbsfleet United"

"Blyth Spartans 1 - 1 Droylsden"

"Cowdenbeath P - P Stenhousemuir"

Commentary on every episode from Des and Tim Gudgin himself, the timeless voice of the English Saturday afternoon. Also includes bonus featurette exploring the infamous Final Score coughing fit of March 20th 1982.

Pay per DVD – just 400 regular payments of £9.99

Try new...

PORN ZERO

All the great porn flavour.

Zero naughtiness.

This tantalising new adult channel from Bravo features all the saucy scenarios from your favourite pornos, but without any of the uncomfortable penetrative bits. Every night from 11pm onwards enjoy 6 whole hours of men successfully installing boilers and fixing cars - exchanging double-entendres until the scantily clad customer is invoiced and sent on her way.

TOTAL FORMULA

Enhance tone. Banish sad. Confirm Betterness.

Try one of our personalised better-for-you formulas:

Podge Burn

Tone Emulsifier

Optimum Maintenance

Reduce Ghastliness

The Power of Love

After the success of "The Carribean Cruise of Sun and Shame (inc. Guantanamo)", and "The 'Off the Wall' Conflict-resolution Absailing off the Israeli West Bank barrier", HOLIdare, the London Shite travel service for those seeking to add some guilty spice to their holiday indulgence, proudly presents something for holiday-makers of a more luxurious disposition...

HOTEL RWANDA

******

A 6-star resort featuring spa, 18-hole golf course and frequent chilling reminders of man's capacity for genocidal fury.

Each room comes with a private butler who is good at telling stories, polishing shoes and carrying trays.

"I've never felt so awful and so comfy."
Rageh Omar

STARCODES

Don't just guess your future, buy it!

AQUARIUS

Popular with feeble male office drones mainly due to the almost guaranteed dalliance with the slightly slutty girl on Reception by the end of the year and a strong possibility of beating your flatmate at Pro Evolution Soccer.

£2.50 

PISCES

Great as a gift for someone who has wronged you of late, Pisces' current affiliation with Mars has angered the traditionalist cadre of the cosmos and they will be looking to instill some discipline. Expect a torrid time in the colon and pancreas and an excessive build-up of earwax.

£5 

LEO

Perfect for the aspiring WAG, Leo is in its 'literal' phase this year meaning you will almost undoubtedly meet with a famous Leo and most likely volunteer sexual congress. Will it be Sayer or Di Caprio? For £1.60 it's worth a punt.

£1.60 

MERCEDES

New to the Zodiac after an agressive take-over of Sagittarius in the summer, Mercedes offers a smooth and reliable life-ride, although you may yearn for more excitement before too long. With talk of further expansion into Saturn and even Jupiter, future prospects look healthy.

£50k 

LIBRA

Balance. Judgement. Calmness. You will have trouble spelling all of these words over the coming weeks, but your mental disintegration will charm those around you.

£9.99 

TAURUS

Jupiter's guilt blends with Saturn's indifference to make for a truly remarkable situation. Everything will start fitting perfectly into place, but just make sure you retain a sense of perspective – for while the planets may be aligned, the Sun does have a tendency to shit all over everything.

£2.20 

CAPRICORN

Great for the kids, Capricorn is destined to have a lot of fun this week and has slim to no chance of being touched inappropriately. Although they will most likely be slightly dehydrated most of the time, they also will learn an important life lesson from a figure of authority or a magician.

£1 

SCORPIO

If you buy one single future from the Starcodes, this really should be it. Not only will you likely discover a hidden talent for filleting fish, but you will also find it in your heart to forgive all those who have hurt you in the past AND find an £2 coin down the back of your sofa.

£99 

GEMINI

If you are naturally a hairless person, Gemini's current acceleration through Mercury's outer consciousness means you should finally be able to grow some sideburns, whether you want them or not.

£4.10 

PILATES

With Mars safely tucked up in bed after last year's furore, it is time for a new start (bear in mind, though, that you are not as attractive as some people tell you). Prepare yourself for fresh challenges and mild food-poisoning.

£10 

MIGHTY WHALE

Unique opportunities lie ahead for you if you select the Mighty Whale. With your birthday falling before Venus' burping season, but after the Moon's special Christmas dance, you are lactose intolerant. Jupiter's deviation through the next cycle will soon change all that.

£1.67 

TEKKEN

An intriguing period of contradictions. Uranus' position on the third floor of the Fourth Solar House suggests you will play a brilliant round of golf in June; but Saturn's insistence on squatting in the Third House tells us that you will lose both your hands in March. Just see how things pan out.

£4.50 

PICTURE CREDITS

Images are listed from left to right and top to bottom (IS = © iStockphoto.com RF = © Rex Features)

INTRODUCTION
p6: IS/Michael Kemter; IS/Jon Schulte; IS/Volodymyr Kudryavtsev; IS/Martin McElligott; IS/Galina Barskaya; p7: IS/Emrah Turudu; IS/Sebastian Kaulitzki.

KNOW
p8: IS/Heiko Bennewitz; Andy Fossum/RF; IS/Alex Mathers; FremantleMedia Ltd/RF; IS/Steve Gray; IS/narvikk; p9: Ron Sachs/RF; IS/Michael Tupy; IS/Jolande Gerritsen; IS/Andrew F Kazmierski; IS/ Sean McDermid; RF; Everett Collection/RF; Greg Mathieson/RF; Lee Thompson/RF; IS/Douglas Allen; p10 IS/ Stefan Klein; Everett Collection/RF; RF; p11: IS/Julie Fisher; IS/Andyd; IS/Dane Steffes; IS/geotrac; IS/Kelly Cline; IS/Michael Kemter; IS/Robert Koopmans; Chris Ratcliffe/RF; RF; Nils Jorgensen/RF; p12: IS/Nathan Maxfield; IS/Stiv Kahlina; IS/Martin Taylor; IS/Selahattin Bayram; IS/luminis; p13: IS/Diane Diederich; IS/blackred; Tony Larkin/RF; FremantleMedia Ltd/RF; p14: IS/Royce DeGrie; RF; Geoffrey Robinson/RF; IS/blackred; Sipa Press/RF; IS/Wayne Pillinger; IS/Eric Simard; IS/pjmorley; IS/Scott Leigh; IS/William Walsh; p16 IS/Igor Terekhov; IS/Jane Pang; NBCUPHOTOBANK/RF; IS/Bruce Lonngren; IS/RainforestAustralia; p17: IS/Enoxh; IS/Gareth Patrick; IS/Lisa F. Young; IS/rusm; IS/Oleg Kulakov; Sipa Press/RF; IS/chimpyk; p18: IS/Milos Luzanin; Sipa Press/RF; Julian Makey/RF; Ken McKay/RF; RF; p19: IS/James Steidl; IS/Roberto Adrian; Jim Smeal/BEI/RF; RF.

BE
p20: IS/Andrzej Burak; IS/Sean Locke; IS/Amanda Rohde; IS/David Pedre p21: IS/Chris Schmidt; IS/Quavondo Nguyen; IS/Kelly Talele; IS/Tyler Stalman; IS/Adam Kazmierski; IS/Rcaliban; p22: IS/blaneyphoto; IS/Jeffrey Smith; p23: IS/Sean Locke; IS/Aliaksandr Stsiazhyn; IS/angelhell; IS/Kayann Legg; IS/Dan Tero; IS/Denis Pepin; IS/Brett Charlton; IS/Mel Stoutsenberger; Woman's Weekly/RF; p24: IS/Milos Luzanin; IS/Robert Churchill; RF; p25: IS/Mark Papas; IS/Scott Waite; IS/James Steidl; IS/druvo; IS/Stock Photo NYC; Mike Daines/RF; RF; Robin Humer/RF; IS/Jon Patton; IS/aldra; RF; RF; p26: IS/Donald Gruener; IS/Nicholas Monu; IS/Kelly Cline; IS/Sandra Nicol; IS/Kronick; IS/Trevor Hunt; IS/Joanne Harris and Daniel Bubnich; IS/Miroslav Ferkuniak; p27: IS/Kevin Russ; IS/istihza; IS/sterlsev; IS/Dale Taylor; RF; p28: IS/Royce DeGrie; IS/Margarita Borodina; RF; IS/Royce DeGrie; IS/DSGpro; IS/Nic Taylor; IS/Lise Gagne; p29: IS/Imad Birkholz; IS/Joan Vicent Cantó Roig; IS/Dena Steiner; IS/Juanmonino; IS/Elena Korenbaum; IS/apashack; IS/Roberto A Sanchez; IS: Sophia Tsibikaki; IS/Eric Foltz; IS/Chris Schmidt; p30: IS/Lise Gagne; IS/Andy Green; IS/Justin Horrocks; IS/Kevin Russ; IS/Neustockimages; p31: IS/Jordan Philips; IS/Jacob Wackerhausen; RF; IS/Chris Schmidt; p32: Matt Baron/BEI/RF; Mimmo Chianura/RF; p33: IS/Ahmet Mert Onengut; IS/Jurie Maree; IS/Robert Churchill; IS/Marilyn Nieves; IS/Dejan Nikolic; IS/Lawrence Sawyer; IS/Evgeny Rannev; IS/Robert Churchill; IS/Alexey Ivanov.

PONDER
p34: Top Photo Group/RF; IS/PhantomOfTheOpera; IS/narvikk; p35: IS/fotoIE; IS/bitter; IS/iofoto; p36: IS/Dzmitry Shpak; RF; IS/Nathan McClunie; IS/Michal Rozanski; RF; p37: IS/Dave White; Sipa Press/RF; Sipa Press/RF; East News/RF; IS/YinYang; p38: Paramount/Everett/RF; IS/Oleg Prikhodko; RF; IS/Jeff McDonald; Mark Leech/RF; p39: Richard Young/RF; Sipa Press/RF; IS/Steven von Niederhausern; IS/Todd Smith; Picture Perfect/RF; Weinstein/Everett /RF; p40: IS/studiovancaspel; James McCauley/RF; RF; IS/XAOC; Alex Segre/RF; IS/Joao Virissimo; IS/Archives; IS/Duncan Walker; p41: IS/Jim Larkin; IS/Milos Luzanin; IS/dirkr; IS/Robert Simon; IS/Bill Grove; IS/Christoph Ermel; IS/Roman Milert; IS/Felix Mökel; p42: IS/Jan Rihak; IS/Serdar Yagci; ITV/RF; Geoff Robinson/RF; IS/Thomas Perkins; David Fisher/RF; p43; p44: IS/Achim Prill; IS/Trevor Hunt; IS/Korhan Hasim Isik; IS/Dale Hogan; IS/Alija; IS/Nathan Jones; p45: IS/Izabela Habur; IS/Jacob Wackerhausen; IS/Tyler Stalman; IS/Florea Marins Catalin; p46: IS/Konstantin Tavrov; IS/Kateryna Davydenko; IS/Sergii Shalimov; IS/Malcolm Romain; RF; IS/Johanna Goodyear; p47: IS/Aldo Murillo; Brian J. Ritchie/RF; IS/Diane Diederich; ITV/RF; IS/ Duncan Walker; RF.

WATCH
p48: IS/Marie-france Bélanger; Stuart Atkins/RF; IS/Sean Locke; IFAW/Stewart Cook/RF; p49: IS/Eva Serrabassa; p50: Donald Cooper/RF; Sipa Press/RF; Stuart Atkins/RF; David Fisher/RF; David Fisher/RF; Alinari/RF; p51: FremantleMedia Ltd/RF; David Fisher/RF; IS/Emrah Turudu; IS/Lawrence Sawyer; James McCauley/RF; RF; IS/Karen Mower; IS/Mikhail Bistrov; p52: IS/Alwyn Cooper; IS/Eric Isselée; Kristin Callahan/RF; IS/Serdar Yagci; IS/Eric Etman; IS/Sunagatov Dmitry; IS/Sophia Tsibikaki; ITV/RF; IS/Roberta Casaliggi; IS/Aleksandr Bondarchiuk; IS/kkgas; IS/sgursozlu; IS/David Kay; IS/Jacob Wackerhausen; Ken McKay/RF; IS/Feng Yu; IS/Jan Rihak; p53: IS/Marie-france Bélanger; IS/Birgitte Magnus; RF; IS/Sharon Dominick; IS/Andrea Skjold; p54: IS/Matjaz Boncina; John Dee/RF; IS/William Day; Sipa Press/RF; IS/Ljupco; IS/Vladislav Lebedinski; p55: IS/poco_bw; IS/Daniel Brunner; IS/Vasiliy Yakobchuk; p56: IS/Ken Cameron; IS/Roman Milert; IS/Valentin Casarsa; IS/Nicholas Homrich; IS/xyno; IS/pederk; IS/Olafur Jon Jonsson; IS/Hakan German; p57: IS/AndyL; IS/cyan22; IS/Chris3fer; IS/Mark Yuill; IS/Terry Wilson; IS/Lisa F. Young; p58: IS/Jacob Wackerhausen; IS/Hal Bergman; IS/Sieto Verver; p59: IS/Rosemarie Gearhart; IS/Douglas Allen; IS/Rudi Tapper; p60: IS/Mustafa Deliormanli; Everett Collection/RF; IS/Maxim Tupikov; IS/OxCreative; IS/Hadrian Kubasiewicz; p61: IS/Joachim Angeltun; IS/Sebastian Kaulitzki.

EAT
p62: IS/bluestocking; IS/bluestocking; p63: Stuart Nimmo/RF; IS/Daniel Timiraos; IS/Anthony Baggett; IS/SweetyMommy; RF; IS/Ivan Mateev; IS/Floortje; Marc Larkin/RF; IS/Archives; Sipa Press/RF; IS/; Laura Neal; p64: IS/Heather Faye Bath; IS/Soubrette; IS/Dave White; IS/Marcelo Wain; IS/Vassiliy Mikhailin; IS/Dobri Dobrinov; IS/bluestocking; IS/Selahattin Bayram; IS/Paul Cowan; p65: Everett Collection/RF; Geoffrey Swaine/RF; IS/Marcel Mooij; IS/Eric Simard; IS/Helder Almeida; IS/4x6; IS/Robert Dant; IS/Devan Muir; IS/Eric Isselée; IS/sasimoto; p66: IS/Marie-france Bélanger; IS/Don Wilkie; IS/blackred; IS/Sebastian Kaulitzi; Sipa Press/RF; p67: IS/Dori OConnell; IS/Alexey Stiop; IS/Lynn Seeden; IS/Erik Lam; p68: IS/Ljupco; IS/Sascha Burkard; IS/Anthony Hall; IS/Luca di Filippo; IS/kaczka; IS/Erik Lam; IS/Jonathan Parry; p69: IS/Dusan Zidar; IS/Maria Toutoudaki; IS/asterix0597; IS/Rob Belknap; IS/Sebastian Kaulitzki; Sipa Press/RF; p70: IS/Pali Rao; IS/Darja Tokranova; IS/Brian Adducci; IS/Juanmonimo; IS/Boris Zaytsev; p71: IS/Kasia Biel; IS/Robert Payne; IS/jallfree; IS/Christian Michael.

TAKE FLIGHT
p72: IS/Dan Chippendale; IS/MBPhoto; IS/James Arrington; p73: IS/HultonArchive; IS/Sherwin McGehee; IS/lushik; p74: IS/poco_bw; IS/John Woodcock; IS/Kevin Russ; Brian Rasic/RF; p75: IS/Tobias Helbig; IS/Heather Wallace; IS/Guenter Guni; p76: IS/Matjaz Boncina; IS/Trevor Hunt; IS/Jan Rysavy; IS/anzeletti; Sipa Press/RF; IS/Nick Schlax; IS/Richard Cliff; IS/Kermarrec Aurelien; IS/PhantomOfTheOpera; Top Photo Group/RF; IS/Branislav Bubanja; p77: IS/Boris Ryzhkov; ITV/RF; IS/ATDA; IS/Blackbeck; p78: IS/Joanne Harris and Daniel Bubnich; IS/TommL; IS/Jon Helgason; IS/Eric Isselée; Ken McKay/RF; p79: IS/scubabartek; IS/Alan McCredie.

SWEAT
p80: Sipa Press/RF; Olycom SPA/RF; p81: IS/Jason Lugo; IS/George Peters; IS/Trevor Hunt; IS/Joachim Angeltun; IS/Devon Stephens; IS/Stefan Klein; IS/Joachim Angeltun; IS/RichVintage; p82: IS/Ryan Meline; IS/Robert Kudera; IS/Paola Canzonetta; IS/Brasil2; IS/Zlatko Kostic; IS/Paola Canzonetta; p83: IS/György Hepka; IS/Paola Canzonetta; IS/Eliza Snow; IS/Paola Canzonetta; IS/morganl; IS/Mark Murphy; IS/Paola Canzonetta; p84: Richard Saker/RF; IS/Emrah Turudu; p85: IS/Dan Tero; Francesco Guidicini/RF; IS/Alexander Kalina; IS/Junji Takemoto; IS/James Allred; IS/Mark Stay; p86: Sipa Press/RF; Justin Downing/RF; P87: IS/SX70; IS/Bojan Fatur; Julian Makey/RF; IS/Bill Noll; IS/Juanmonimo; IS/Joe Gough; IS/Julie Masson Deshaies; IS/Eric Isselée.

CLASSIFIEDS
p88: IS/plains; IS/Rebecca Ellis; IS/JoeLena; IS/Mustafa Deliormanli; p89: IS/Julie Fisher; IS/Michael Kemter; IS/Dan Brandenburg; p90: IS/Manuel Velasco; IS/Michael Kemter; IS/Sebastien Bergeron; p91: IS/Darren Baker; p92: IS/Geoffrey Holman; IS/Matthew Cole; IS/SweetyMommy; IS/Andrew Howe; IS/Steve Luker; IS/Effinity Stock Photography; IS/Andrew Reh; IS/Ramona Heim; p93: IS/Tjanze; IS/Grigory Bibikov; ITV/RF; IS/DIGIcal; p94: IS/Studiovitra; IS/Stila Goh; IS/Drazen Vukelic; IS/David Kahn; IS/Guenter Guni; RF; IS/Robert Latawiec; IS/Bubaone.